/05

BEGINNING WORKBOOK

THE OXFORD
Picture
Dictionary

Canadian Edition

MARJORIE FUCHS

Canadian adaptation by

OXFO

UNIVERSITY

OXFORD
UNIVERSITY PRESS

70 Wynford Drive, Don Mills, Ontario M3C 1J9
www.oup.com/ca

Oxford University Press is a department of the University of Oxford.
It furthers the University's objective of excellence in research, scholarship,
and education by publishing worldwide in

Oxford New York
Auckland Bangkok Buenos Aires Cape Town Chennai
Dar es Salaam Delhi Hong Kong Istanbul Karachi Kolkata
Kuala Lumpur Madrid Melbourne Mexico City Mumbai Nairobi
São Paulo Shanghai Taipei Tokyo Toronto

Oxford is a trade mark of Oxford University Press
in the UK and in certain other countries

ISBN 0-19-541468-3

Canadian Cataloguing in Publication Data

Fuchs, Marjorie, 1949-
  The Oxford picture dictionary, Canadian edition.
  Beginning workbook

ISBN 0-19-541468-3

1. Picture dictionaries, English – Problems, exercises, etc.
2. English language – Textbooks for second language learners.*
I. Grennan, Maggie, 1956- . II. Shapiro, Norma. Oxford picture
dictionary: monolingual. III. Title.

PE1629.S49 1999 Suppl. 1   423'.1   C98-933044-3

Editorial Manager: Susan Lanzano
Editor: Lynne Barsky
Production Editor: Klaus Jekeli
Art Director: Lynn Luchetti
Design Project Manager: Susan Brorein
Designer: Shelley Himmelstein
Art Buyer: Patricia Marx
Cover design production: Brett Sonnenschein
Picture Researcher: Clare Maxwell
Production Manager: Abram Hall
Cover design by Silver Editions

Printing (last digit): 10 9 8 7 6 5

Printed in Canada.

Acknowledgements

The publisher and author would like to thank the following reviewers for their help throughout the development of the workbooks:

Glenda Adamson, Lubie G. Alatriste, Leor Alcalay, Fiona Armstrong, Jean Barlow, Margrajean Bonilla, Susan Burke, Becky Carle, Bev Clausner, Analee Doney, Laurie Ehrenhalt, Michele Epstein, Christine Evans, Lynn A. Freeland, Carole Goodman, Joyce Grabowski, Esther Greenwell, Kelly Gutierrez, Christine Hill, Leann Howard, Lori Howard, Hilary Jarvis, Nanette Kafka, Cliff Ker, Margaret Lombard, Carol S. McLain, Monica Miele, Patsy Mills, Debra L. Mullins, Dian Perkins, Barbara Jane Pers, Marianne Riggiola, Virginia Robbins, Linda Susan Robinson, Michele Rodgers-Amini, Maria Salinas, Jimmy E. Sandifer, Jeffrey Scofield, Ann Silverman, Susan A. Slavin, Peggy Stubbs, Lynn Sweeden, Christine Tierney, Laura L. Webber

In addition, the author would like to thank the following people:

Susan Lanzano, Editorial Manager, for overseeing a huge and complex project of which the *Workbooks* were just a part. She orchestrated the entire project without losing sight of the individual components.

Lynne Barsky, Editor, for four years of hard work and dedication, from the all-important initial research to the scrutinizing of final copy and art. I appreciate Lynne's calm and upbeat steadfastness throughout the project.

Klaus Jekeli, Production Editor, for applying his intelligent, keen eye to the manuscript and art, assuring that everything worked together.

Norma Shapiro and Jayme Adelson-Goldstein, authors of the *Dictionary,* and Shirley Brod, editor of the *Teacher's Book,* for meticulously reviewing the manuscript and offering particularly helpful feedback and enthusiastic support.

Eliza Jensen and Amy Cooper, senior editors, for looking at the manuscript at important junctures and offering sage advice.

Margo Bonner, my coauthor of the *Intermediate Workbook,* for her very valuable feedback during the developmental phase of this project and for her insightful critique of the manuscript.

The design team for making me feel welcome at their meetings, and for giving me the chance to see the huge amount of work and creativity they put into the project long after the manuscript had been submitted.

Rick Smith, as always, for his unswerving support and for his insightful comments on all aspects of the project. Once again, he proved to be equally at home in both the world of numbers and the world of words.

To the Teacher

The *Beginning Workbook* and the *Intermediate Workbook* that accompany *The Oxford Picture Dictionary, Canadian Edition,* have been designed to provide meaningful and enjoyable practice of the vocabulary that students are learning. These workbooks supply high-interest contexts and real information for enrichment and self-expression.

Both *Workbooks* conveniently correspond page-for-page to the 140 topics of the *Picture Dictionary.* For example, if you are working on page 22 in the *Dictionary,* the activities for this topic, Age and Physical Description, will be found on page 22 in the *Workbook.*

All topics in the *Beginning Workbook* follow the same easy-to-use format. Exercise 1 is always a "look in your dictionary" activity where students are asked to complete a task while looking in their *Picture Dictionary.* The tasks include answering questions about the pictures, judging statements true or false, counting the number of illustrated occurrences of a vocabulary item, completing a timeline, or speculating about who said what.

Following this activity are one or more content-rich contextualized exercises, including true or false, matching, labelling, fill-in-the-blanks, multiple choice, rank ordering, categorizing, odd-one-out, and completion of forms. These exercises often feature graphs and charts with real data for students to work with as they practice the new vocabulary. Many topics include a personalization exercise that asks "What about you?" where students can use the new vocabulary to give information about their own lives or to express their opinions.

The final exercise for each topic is a "Challenge" which can be assigned to students for additional work in class or as homework. Challenge activities provide higher level speaking and writing practice, and for some topics will require students to interview classmates, conduct surveys, or find information outside of class. For example on page 37, the Challenge for the topic Apartments asks students to look at a local newspaper, choose an apartment ad, and describe the apartment.

Each of the 12 units ends with "Another Look," a review which allows students to practice vocabulary from all of the topics of a unit in a game or puzzle-like activity, such as picture crosswords, word searches, and C-searches, where students search in a picture for items which begin with the letter *c.* These activities are at the back of the *Beginning Workbook* on pages 170–181.

Throughout both the *Beginning* and the *Intermediate Workbooks,* vocabulary is carefully controlled and recycled. Students should, however, be encouraged to use their *Picture Dictionaries* to look up words that they do not recall or, if they are doing topics out of sequence, may not yet have learned.

The *Oxford Picture Dictionary Workbooks* can be used in the classroom or at home for self-study. An *Answer Key* is included at the back of both *Workbooks.*

I hope you and your students enjoy using these workbooks as much as I have enjoyed writing them.

M.F.

To the Student

The Oxford Picture Dictionary, Canadian Edition, has more than 3700 words. This workbook will help you use them in your daily life.

• It's easy to use! The *Workbook* pages match the pages in your *Picture Dictionary.* For example, to practice the words on page 22 in your *Picture Dictionary,* go to page 22 in your *Workbook.*

• It has exercises you will enjoy. Some exercises show real information. A bar graph of people's favourite colours is on page 12, and a chart showing the top 10 pets in North America is on page 133. Another exercise, which asks "What about you?" gives you a chance to use your

own information. You'll find stories, puzzles, and conversations, too.

At the end of each topic there is a Challenge, a chance to use your new vocabulary more independently. And finally, every unit has a one-page summary, called Another Look, in a section at the back of the book. This is a game or puzzle activity that practises the vocabulary from an entire unit.

Learning new words is both challenging and fun. I had a lot of fun writing this workbook. I hope you enjoy using it!

M.F.

Contents

1. Everyday Language

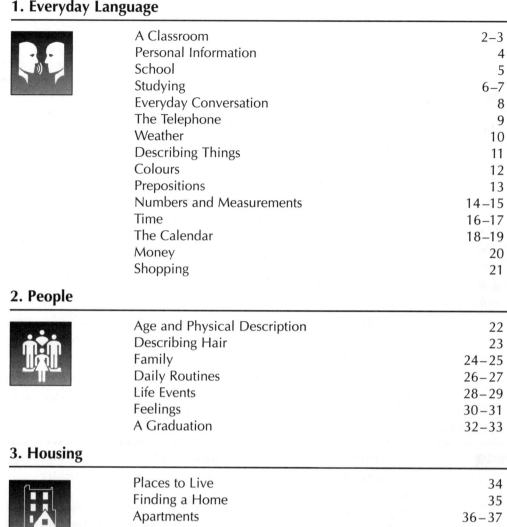

2. People

3. Housing

4. Food

Contents

A Classroom

1. Look at the classroom in your dictionary. How many … are there?

   a. teachers   <u> 1 </u>   **c.** students   <u>   </u>   **e.** globes   <u>   </u>

   b. computers <u>   </u>   **d.** cassette players <u>   </u>   **f.** maps   <u>   </u>

2. Look at the list of school supplies. Check (✔) the items you see on the table.

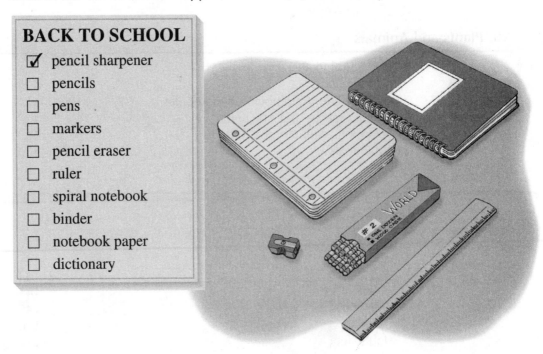

BACK TO SCHOOL

- ☑ pencil sharpener
- ☐ pencils
- ☐ pens
- ☐ markers
- ☐ pencil eraser
- ☐ ruler
- ☐ spiral notebook
- ☐ binder
- ☐ notebook paper
- ☐ dictionary

3. Correct this student's spelling test.

Spelling Test

1. screen	6. eraser
2. overhead pro*j*ector	7. alfabet
3. computter	8. map
4. clock	9. bookkase
5. chawk	10. bulletin bord

4. Match the instructions with the pictures. Write the number.

<u>8</u> a. Listen to the cassette.

___ b. Open your workbooks.

___ c. Write the numbers on the board.

___ d. Please stand up.

___ e. Please take out your pencils.

___ f. Erase the chalkboard, please.

___ g. Please close your workbooks.

___ h. Put away your pencils.

___ i. Please take a seat.

___ j. Write the alphabet on the board.

1.

2.

3.

4.

5.

6.

7.

8.

9.

10.

5. What about you? Check (✔) the items you use in your classroom.

☐ pencils
☐ pens
☐ markers
☐ pencil sharpener
☐ pencil eraser

☐ dictionary
☐ picture dictionary
☐ spiral notebook
☐ workbook
☐ textbook

☐ notebook paper
☐ binder
☐ ruler
☐ cassette player
☐ Other: _____

Challenge Write about the items in Exercise 5. **Example:** *I have one dictionary. I have two pens. I don't have any pencils.*

3

Personal Information

1. Look in your dictionary. What is Sam Larson's...?
   a. postal code   <u>V6B 5G3</u>   **c.** apartment #   <u>   </u>

   b. area code   <u>   </u>   **d.** Social Insurance # <u>   </u>

2. Match the personal information words with the examples. Write the number.

   <u>6</u> **a.** middle initial   **1.** female

   <u>   </u> **b.** signature   **2.** Ontario

   <u>   </u> **c.** city   **3.** (416)

   <u>   </u> **d.** sex   **4.** 432 123 456

   <u>   </u> **e.** area code   **5.** Toronto

   <u>   </u> **f.** Social Insurance number   **6.** S.

   <u>   </u> **g.** name   **7.** A1B 2C4

   <u>   </u> **h.** postal code   **8.** *Miriam S. Shakter*

   <u>   </u> **i.** province   **9.** Miriam S. Shakter

3. What about you? Fill out the form. Use your own information.

Last name_____	First name_____ Middle initial_____
Sex ☐ male ☐ female	
Place of birth_____	Date of birth_____
	(month) (date) (year)
Address_____	Apt. #_____
_____ _____	
(city)	(province) (postal code)
Telephone (_____) _____	
_____	_____
Signature	Social Insurance #

Challenge   Interview a classmate. Find out his or her last name, first name, middle initial, address, and place of birth. Write the information on your own paper.

1. Look in your dictionary. Put the words in the correct column.

PEOPLE	PLACES	
teacher	classroom	
_____	_____	_____
_____	_____	_____
_____	_____	_____
	_____	_____
	_____	_____
	_____	_____

2. Look at the floor plan. Complete the directory.

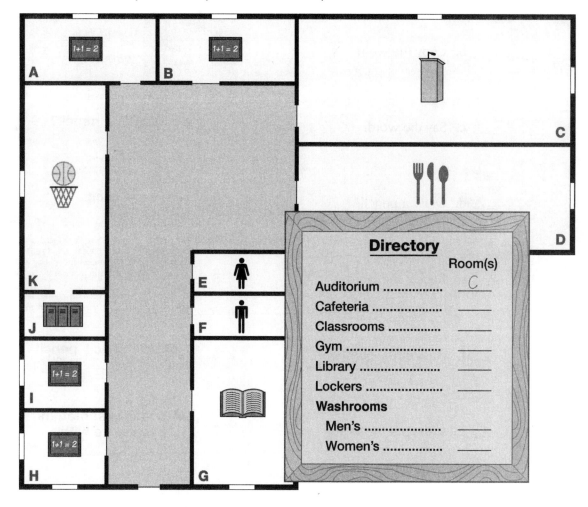

Directory

	Room(s)
Auditorium	_C_
Cafeteria	___
Classrooms	___
Gym	___
Library	___
Lockers	___
Washrooms	
Men's	___
Women's	___

3. What about you? Check (✓) the items your school has.

☐ an auditorium   ☐ a library   ☐ a track   ☐ a counsellor's office   ☐ a cafeteria

Challenge Draw a floor plan or write a directory for your school.

5

1. Look in your dictionary. **True** or **False**?

   a. Picture A: The woman is dictating a sentence.   _____False_____

   b. Picture I: The men are sharing a book.   _____

   c. Picture K: The group is discussing a story.   _____

   d. Picture P: The students are talking with each other.   _____

   e. Picture Q: The student is correcting papers.   _____

2. Match the instructions with the responses. Write the number.

_3_ **a.** Ask a question.   **1.** P - E - N - C - I - L

____ **b.** Copy the word.   **2.** pencil / pencil

____ **c.** Say the word.   **3.** What's a pencil?

____ **d.** Draw a pencil.   **4.** Pencil.

____ **e.** Repeat the word.   **5.**
pence /pens/ *n.* (*pl.*) pennies.
pencil /'pensl/ *n.* instrument for writing and drawing, made of a thin piece of wood with lead inside it.
penetrate /'penɪtreɪt/ *v.* go into or through something: *A nail penetrated the car tire.*

____ **f.** Answer the question.   **6.** pencil pencil pencil

____ **g.** Cross out the word.   **7.** A pencil is something you write with.

____ **h.** Look up the word.   **8.**

____ **i.** Spell the word.   **9.** pencil

6

3. Complete this test.

Name:_____ Class:_____

1. Fill in the blanks. Use the words in the box.

~~in~~   out   up

a. I'm filling ___in___ the blanks.
b. The students are looking _____ new words in the dictionary.
c. The teacher is passing _____ the papers.

2. Cross out the word that doesn't belong.
a. help   share   ~~match~~
b. spell   underline   circle
c. draw   talk   copy

3. Underline the words that begin with *s*. Circle the words that begin with *c*.
read   (copy)   say   share   help   circle   check   spell

4. Put the words in question 3 in alphabetical order.
___check___
_____
_____
_____
_____
_____
_____
_____

5. Match.
__3__ a. Spell   **1.** a picture.
____ b. Draw   **2.** a question
____ c. Ask   **3.** a word.

4. What about you? Look in your dictionary. Which classroom activities do you like? Which activities don't you like? Make two lists on your own paper.

Challenge Look up the word *thimble* in your picture dictionary.
a. Write the word: _____   c. Draw a picture of a thimble.
b. Write the page number: _____

7

Everyday Conversation

1. Look in your dictionary. Match the parts of the conversations. Write the number.

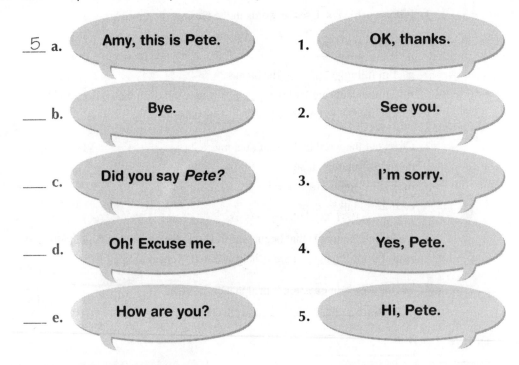

_5_ **a.** Amy, this is Pete.

1. OK, thanks.

___ **b.** Bye.

2. See you.

___ **c.** Did you say *Pete?*

3. I'm sorry.

___ **d.** Oh! Excuse me.

4. Yes, Pete.

___ **e.** How are you?

5. Hi, Pete.

2. Circle the correct words.

a. John introduces his friend:

> Hello.
> Hi, I'm Ming.
> (Ming, this is Kim.)

b. Ming makes sure he understands:

> Oh! Excuse me.
> How are things?
> Did you say *Kim?*

c. Ming begins a conversation:

> See you.
> Good night.
> How are things?

d. John compliments Ming:

> That's a great jacket.
> See you.
> Thank you.

e. Ming thanks John:

> I'm sorry.
> Thank you.
> Fine, thanks.

f. Ming ends the conversation:

> Good evening.
> Good morning.
> See you.

Challenge Look at **page 182** in this book. Complete the conversation.

1. Look in your dictionary. Match the numbers with the words.

  _4_ **a.** 555-2134   **1.** long-distance call

  ____ **b.** 1 (401) 543-4323   **2.** emergency service

  ____ **c.** 411   **3.** operator

  ____ **d.** 0   **4.** local call

  ____ **e.** 011-57-1-555-3456   **5.** directory assistance

  ____ **f.** 911   **6.** international call

2. Put the sentences in the correct order. Then fill in the blank.

> ### Instructions for a _____ phone
>
> ____ **a.** Listen for the dial tone.   ____ **d.** Deposit coins.
> _1_ **b.** Pick up the receiver.   ____ **e.** Hang up the receiver.
> ____ **c.** Leave a message.   ____ **f.** Dial the number.

3. Complete the ad. Use the words in the box.

answering machine
cellular phone
cordless phone
pager
~~phone~~

a. _phone_
black, white, beige

b. _____

c. _____   **d.** _____   **e.** _____

25-Channel

4. What about you? Complete the phone numbers for your city or town.

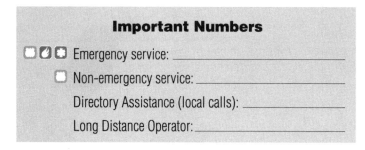

> ### Important Numbers
>
> Emergency service: _____
> Non-emergency service: _____
> Directory Assistance (local calls): _____
> Long Distance Operator: _____

Challenge   Find out the area codes for five cities. Look in a phone book or ask your classmates.
Example: *Edmonton—403*

Weather

1. Look in your dictionary. Describe the temperature.

   Celsius: 25° _____   -10° _____   40° _____

2. Look at the weather map. Check (✓) the statements that are true.

☐ **a.** It's raining in Saskatoon.

☑ **b.** There's a snowstorm in Yellowknife.

☐ **c.** Labrador is having freezing rain.

☐ **d.** It's windy in Ottawa.

☐ **e.** It's freezing in Winnipeg.

☐ **f.** It's raining in St. John's.

☐ **g.** It's icy in Québec City.

☐ **h.** It's sunny but freezing in Whitehorse.

☐ **i.** It's hot and sunny in Windsor.

☐ **j.** It's sunny and warm in Vancouver.

3. What about you? What kinds of weather do you like? Check (✓) the columns.

	I LIKE IT	IT'S OK	I DON'T LIKE IT
humid			
cool and foggy			
rainy			
warm and windy			
Other:			

Challenge Write a weather report for your city. **Example:** *Monday, January 25. Today it's sunny and warm in Victoria. The temperature is…*

10

1. Look in your dictionary. Write the opposites.

   a. big   __little__   **d.** cheap   _____

   b. fat   _____   **e.** ugly   _____

   c. heavy   _____   **f.** slow   _____

2. Look at the picture of the classroom.

True or **False**? Change the <u>underlined</u> words in the false sentences. Make the sentences true.

   a. The classroom is <u>noisy</u>.   __False. The classroom is quiet.__

   b. There's a <u>big</u> clock in the room.   _____

   c. Bob is a <u>good</u> student.   _____

   d. The teacher's desk is <u>messy</u>.   _____

   e. The bookcase is <u>neat</u>.   _____

   f. The words on the board are <u>easy</u>.   _____

   g. The chairs are <u>soft</u>.   _____

3. What about you? Check (✔) the words that describe your classroom.

   ☐ beautiful   ☐ big   ☐ cold   ☐ hot   ☐ messy

   ☐ neat   ☐ noisy   ☐ quiet   ☐ ugly   ☐ Other: _____

Challenge   Describe your classroom. Write eight sentences.

Colours

1. Look at **page 3** in your dictionary. What colour is the...?

   a. binder ___green___

   b. spiral notebook _____

   c. textbook _____

   d. ruler _____

2. Look at the bar graph. Put the colours in order. (Number 1 = their favourite)

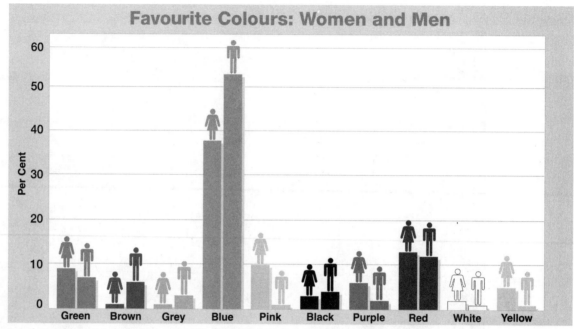

Favourite Colours: Women and Men

Based on information from: Weiss, D.: *The Great Divide: How Females & Males Really Differ.*
(NY: Poseidon Press, 1991)

WOMEN'S FAVOURITE COLOURS

1. ___blue___
2. _____
3. _____
4. _____
5. _____
6. _____
7. _____
8. _____
9. _____ and _____

MEN'S FAVOURITE COLOURS

1. _____
2. _____
3. _____
4. _____
5. _____
6. _____
7. _____
8. _____, _____, and _____

3. What about you? Put the colours in order. (Number 1 = your favourite)

   ___ red   ___ green   ___ purple   ___ light blue   ___ orange

   ___ yellow   ___ pink   ___ brown   ___ dark blue   ___ beige

Challenge Make a list of the colours in Exercise 2. Ask five women and five men to put the colours in order. (Number 1 = their favourite) Do their answers agree with the information in Exercise 2?

1. Look in your dictionary. **True** or **False**?

   a. The black box is on a shelf.   _____True_____

   b. The white box is under the black box.   _____

   c. The purple box is next to the pink box.   _____

   d. The grey box is behind the turquoise box.   _____

   e. The red box is near the yellow box.   _____

2. Read the sentences. Fill in the blanks.

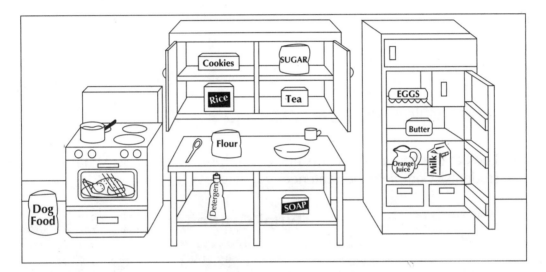

   a. The box of cookies is o__ the shelf.

   b. The box of rice is on the shelf b_ _ _ _ the cookies.

   c. The tea is n_ _ _ to the rice, to the right.

   d. The sugar is on the shelf a_ _ _ _ the tea.

   e. The bag of flour is b_ _ _ _ _ _ the bowl and the spoon.

   f. The milk is on the shelf u_ _ _ _ the butter.

   g. The dog food is b_ _ _ _ _ the stove.

   h. The orange juice is beside the milk, to the l_ _ _ .

   i. There is a chicken i__ the oven.

Challenge   Draw a picture of your classroom. Write about the locations of the classroom items in your picture. **Example:** *The map is next to the board, on the right.*

Numbers and Measurements

1. Look in your dictionary. What kinds of numbers are these?

   a. thirty <u>cardinal</u>   **c.** III _____   **e.** 3% _____

   b. 1/3 _____   **d.** thirteenth _____   **f.** thirteen _____

2. Complete the chart.

WORD	NUMBER	ROMAN NUMERAL
ten	10	X
		III
	15	
		L
	20	
one hundred		
		D
one thousand		

3. Look at the bar graph. Ana is first (= the best) in her class. What about the other students? Complete the sentences.

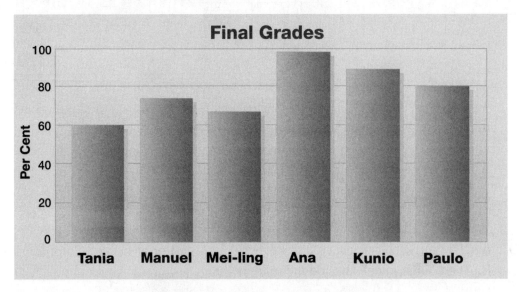

Final Grades

   a. Ana is <u>first</u> in her class.   **d.** Kunio is _____.

   b. Manuel is _____.   **e.** Tania is _____.

   c. Mei-ling is _____.   **f.** Paulo is _____.

4. Complete the pie chart with numbers from the box. Then complete the sentences. Write the per cents in words.

| | ~~50~~ | 25 | 10 | 10 | 5 |

First Languages in Mrs. Rivera's Class
(Percentage of Students)

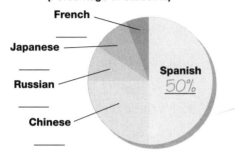

a.   <u>Fifty per cent</u>   speak Spanish.

b.   _____ speak Chinese.

c.   _____ speak French.

d.   _____ speak Russian.

e.   _____ speak Japanese.

5. Look at the books. Complete the sentences. Use fractions in words.

a.   <u>One-fourth</u>   of the books are in Chinese.

b.   _____ are in English.

c.   _____ are in Spanish.

d.   _____ are in either English or Russian.

6. What about you? Measure a bookshelf in school or at home. Complete the chart.

METRES AND CENTIMETRES	
width	
height	
depth	

Challenge How many students in your class speak your language? How many students speak other languages? Calculate the per cents. **Example:** *There are twenty students in my class. Ten students speak Spanish. That's fifty per cent.*

Time

1. Look in your dictionary. What's another way to say…?

    a. ten-thirty   <u>half past ten</u>   **c.** a quarter after three _____

    b. two forty-five _____   **d.** twenty after six   _____

2. Match the numbers with the words.

    <u>3</u> **a.** 3:00   **1.** It's ten to nine.

    ___ **b.** 5:25   **2.** It's a quarter to seven.

    ___ **c.** 2:30   **3.** It's three o'clock.

    ___ **d.** 6:45   **4.** It's a quarter past six.

    ___ **e.** 8:50   **5.** It's a quarter to six.

    ___ **f.** 6:15   **6.** It's two-thirty.

    ___ **g.** 9:10   **7.** It's five twenty-five.

    ___ **h.** 5:45   **8.** It's ten after nine.

3. Complete the clocks.

    4:10

    a. ten after four   **b.** half past six   **c.** eight o'clock   **d.** a quarter to twelve

4. What about you? Answer the questions. Use words and numbers.

    Example: What time is it? It's <u>four-fifteen p.m. (4:15 p.m.)</u> .

    a. What time is it? It's _____ (_____) .

    b. What time is your class? From _____ (_____) to

    _____ (_____) .

5. Look in your dictionary. In which time zone is…?

    a. Caracas   <u>Atlantic</u>   **c.** Denver   _____

    b. Chicago   _____   **d.** Vancouver   _____

6. Look at the chart.

At 12:00 noon, Eastern Standard Time, the time in … is …

Athens	7 P.M.	**Mexico City**	11 A.M.
Baghdad	8 P.M.	**Montreal**	12 N
Bangkok	12 M	**New York City**	12 N
Barcelona	6 P.M.	**Panama**	12 N
Buenos Aires	2 P.M.	**Paris**	6 P.M.
Calcutta	10:30 P.M.	**Rio de Janeiro**	2 P.M.
Frankfurt	6 P.M.	**Riyadh**	8 P.M.
Halifax	1 P.M.	**Rome**	6 P.M.
Hanoi	1 A.M.*	**St. Petersburg**	8 P.M.
Havana	12 N	**San Juan**	12 N
Hong Kong	1 A.M.*	**Seoul**	2 A.M.*
Houston	11 A.M.	**Sydney**	3 A.M.*
London	5 P.M.	**Tel Aviv**	7 P.M.
Los Angeles	9 A.M.	**Tokyo**	2 A.M.*
Mecca	8 P.M.	**Zurich**	6 P.M.

* = the next day   M = midnight   N = noon

It's noon in New York. What time is it in…? Use numbers and the words in the box.

in the morning   in the afternoon   in the evening
at night   noon   midnight

    a. Athens   <u>7:00 in the evening</u>   **g.** St. Petersburg _____

    b. London   _____   **h.** Bangkok _____

    c. Calcutta   _____   **i.** Mexico City _____

    d. Panama   _____   **j.** Frankfurt _____

    e. Halifax   _____   **k.** Los Angeles _____

    f. Tokyo   _____   **l.** Hanoi _____

7. What about you? Does your country of origin have…? Write **Yes** or **No**.

    a. different time zones   _____   **b.** daylight saving time   _____

Challenge Look in your dictionary. Which cities from the chart in Exercise 6 are in the eight time zones pictured? List them for each zone. **Example:** *eastern time: Havana, Montreal,…*

1. Look in your dictionary. In January, 2001, how many … are there?

   a. days ___31___   d. weekdays _____
   b. Mondays _____   e. weekends _____
   c. Thursdays _____   f. full weeks _____

2. Look at Antonio's calendar. **True** or **False**?

S	M	T	W	T	F	S
	1 Science Lab English	**2** Computer Lab Math	**3** English	**4** Gym Math	**5** Language Lab English	**6** To Calgary!
7 Daylight Saving Time!	**8**	**9** N O	**10** C L A S	**11** S E S	**12** To N.Y.	**13** Ana 7:00 P.M.
14	**15** Science Lab English	**16** Auditorium 2:00 Math	**17** English	**18** Gym Math	**19** Language Lab English	**20** Track & Field
21 Mary 6:00 P.M.	**22** Science Lab English	**23** Counsellor's Office 3:15 Math	**24** English	**25** Gym Math	**26** Language Lab English	**27** Library with Frank
28	**29** Science Lab	**30**				

TODAY'S DATE

   a. Antonio has class every day this month. ___False___
   b. He has English twice a week. _____
   c. He was in New York last weekend. _____
   d. Tomorrow he has track and field. _____
   e. Yesterday was Tuesday. _____
   f. He sees Mary Sunday night. _____
   g. He sees her every weekend. _____
   h. There were no classes last week. _____
   i. Daylight saving time begins this week. _____
   j. Next week Antonio sees the school counsellor. _____

3. What about you? Make a calendar of <u>your</u> monthly activities. Write ten sentences.

4. Put these months in the correct seasons. Use your dictionary for help.

| ~~April~~ October January February |
| November July May August |

WINTER   SPRING   SUMMER   FALL

_____   ___April___   _____   _____

_____   _____ _____   _____

5. Match the photos with the captions. Write the letter.

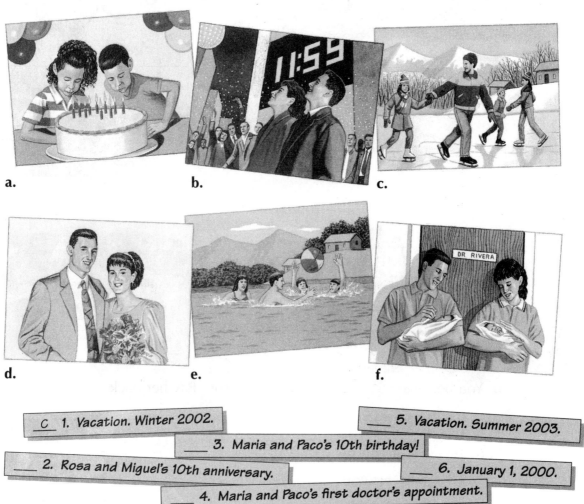

a.   b.   c.

d.   e.   f.

_C_ 1. Vacation. Winter 2002.

____ 5. Vacation. Summer 2003.

____ 3. Maria and Paco's 10th birthday!

____ 2. Rosa and Miguel's 10th anniversary.

____ 6. January 1, 2000.

____ 4. Maria and Paco's first doctor's appointment.

6. What about you? Complete the chart on your own paper.

	BIRTHDAY MONTH	DAY	ANNIVERSARY MONTH	DAY
Your name: _____				
Classmate's name: _____				
Classmate's name: _____				

Challenge Bring some photos to class. Write captions on your own paper.

19

Money

1. Look in your dictionary. How much money is there in…? (Do not include **Ways to pay.**)

   a. coins __$3.41__   **b.** bills _____   **c.** coins and bills _____

2. Look at the money. How much is it? Use numbers.

   a. ____$5.10____   **b.** $ _____ or _____ ¢

   c. _____ or _____   **d.** _____

   e. _____   **f.** _____

3. You borrowed $25.00 from Mary Johnson. Pay her back.

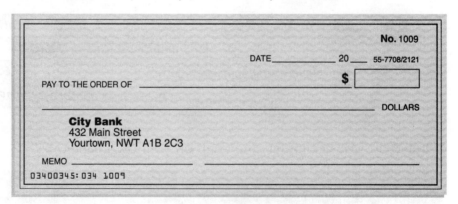

   Check (✓) the form of payment.

   ☐ cash   ☐ traveller's cheque   ☐ personal cheque   ☐ money order

Challenge Look at **page 182** in this book. Answer the questions.

1. Look in your dictionary. Circle the correct words to complete the sentences.

    a. The woman is shopping for two / (three) sweaters.

    b. The regular price / sale price is $9.99.

    c. The change / total is $32.07.

    d. There is / is no sales tax.

    e. The woman gives / sells the sweaters to her daughters.

    f. One of the daughters returns / keeps the red sweater.

    g. One of the daughters exchanges the blue / green sweater.

2. Complete the shopping tips. Use the words in the box.

change	exchange	keep	pay	price
~~receipt~~	return	sales		

BE A $MART $HOPPER

★ Check the price .

★ Get a ___receipt___ .
       a.

    Is the _____ on the receipt correct?
          b.

    Is the _____ tax correct?
          c.

★ If you _____ by cash, count your _____ .
         d.   **e.**

★ Ask:

    Can I _____ this for something else?
          f.

    Can I _____ this for cash?
          g.

★ _____ your receipt.
    h.

3. What about you? Is there sales tax on clothing in your province? _____
If yes, how much is it? _____ %

Challenge Look at **page 183** in this book. Complete the sales slip.

▶ **Go to page 170 for Another Look (Unit 1).**

Age and Physical Description

1. Look at the top of the page in your dictionary. How many … do you see?

   a. people ___9___   **b.** children _____   **c.** teenagers _____   **d.** adults _____

2. Read the ads. Circle all the words that describe age and physical description. Who wrote the ads? Match the ads with the photos. Write the letter.

   _c_ **1.** (Tall) and (Attractive)—middle-aged man of (average weight) seeks friend for travel and sports. 3759 ✉ ☎

   ___ **2.** **Attractive**—slim, elderly woman with many interests seeks relationship with kind, honest man. 3145 ☎

   ___ **3.** **Hi!**—I'm a short, cute, 30-year-old woman. You're smart, nice, and funny. Physical appearance not important. 3945

   ___ **4.** **Short and Sweet**—18-year-old of average weight seeks nice fun-loving man. Photo please. 3296 ✉ ☎

   ___ **5.** **Something Special**—I'm a young, physically challenged man looking for someone to share the great things in life with. 3623 ☎

   ___ **6.** **A Great Guy**—heavyset, friendly and fun. Looking for a happy woman who loves life. 3567 ✉ ☎

   a.   b.

   c.   d.

   e.   f.

3. What about you? Describe one of your friends. Circle the correct words.

   My friend's name is _____.

He's / She's	a / an	short / average height / tall	thin / average weight / heavyset	young / middle-aged / elderly	man. / woman. / boy. / girl.

Challenge Find a picture of a person in a newspaper, magazine, or your dictionary. Write a description.

1. Look at the top picture in your dictionary. How many … do you see?

   a. green rollers   _2_

   b. combs   _____

   c. blow dryers   _____

   d. brushes   _____

   e. hair stylists   _____

   f. scissors   _____

2. Look at the pictures of Cindi. Check (✔) the things that The Hair Salon did to Cindi's hair. Then circle the correct words to complete the paragraph.

   Before

   Now

   The Hair Salon

   ☑ cut
   ☐ set
   ☐ colour
   ☐ perm

   Cindi is very happy with her new hair style. She now has long / short hair.
   a.

   straight / wavy, brown / blond hair. She
   b.   **c.**

   also has a part / bangs. Cindi looks great.
   d.

3. What about you? Draw a picture of a friend's hair. Describe it.

   Example:

   My friend has _shoulder-length_ , _curly_ ,
   red hair.

   My friend has _____, _____,
   _____ hair.

   Check (✔) the correct boxes. He/she has….

   ☐ a part   ☐ bangs   ☐ a moustache   ☐ a beard   ☐ sideburns

---

Challenge   Find pictures of three hair styles in a newspaper, magazine, or your dictionary. Write descriptions.

Family

1. Look at page 24 in your dictionary. Put the words in the correct category.

~~brother~~	cousin	daughter	grandmother	
husband	niece	parent	son	uncle

MALE	FEMALE	MALE OR FEMALE
brother	_____	_____
_____	_____	_____
_____	_____	
_____		

2. Look at page 24 in your dictionary. **True** or **False**?

a. Tom has two sisters. _____False_____

b. Min is Lu's wife. _____

c. Daniel is Min and Lu's nephew. _____

d. Tom and Emily have the same grandparents. _____

e. Rose is Emily's aunt. _____

f. Marta is Eddie's mother-in-law. _____

g. Sara is Berta and Mario's granddaughter. _____

h. Felix is Alice's cousin. _____

i. Ana is Carlos's sister-in-law. _____

j. Tito is Berta and Mario's son-in-law. _____

3. What about you? Complete the form.

Your name:_____

Mother's name:_____ Father's name:_____

Marital status: ☐ single ☐ married ☐ divorced

If married, what is your husband's/wife's name?_____

Do you have any children? ☐ yes ☐ no

If yes, what are their names?_____

4. Look at page 25 in your dictionary. Circle the correct answer.

    a. Carol is Dan's (former wife)/ sister.

    b. Sue is Kim's stepmother / mother.

    c. Rick is a single father / father.

    d. David is Mary's brother / half brother.

    e. Lisa is Bill's half sister / stepsister.

    f. Dan is Bill and Kim's father / stepfather.

5. Look at Megan's story.

Put these sentences about Megan in the correct time order.

___ She's remarried.	___ She's a stepmother.	_1_ She's married.
___ She has a baby.	___ She's a single mother.	___ She's divorced.

6. Complete Nicole's story. Use the information in Exercise 5.

> *Sept. 10, 2002*
>
> Name: Nicole Parker
> My name is Nicole. My ____mother____ 's name is Megan.
>   a.
> My _____'s name is Chet. I have a _____.
>   b.   c.
> His name is Brian. Brian has a _____.
>   d.
> His name is Jason. Jason is my_____.
>   e.

Challenge Draw your family tree. Use the family trees in your dictionary as a model.

Daily Routines

1. Look in your dictionary. Complete Dan Lim's schedule.

6:00	wake up
	get dressed
7:00	
7:30	
	drive to work
5:00	
	pick up the children
	have dinner
8:00	
8:30	
	go to sleep

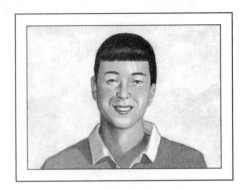

2. Look at the Lims' things. Match each item with the correct activity. Write the letter.

To Do

f 1. go to the market

___ 2. clean the house

___ 3. take the bus

___ 4. make lunch

___ 5. watch TV

___ 6. read the paper

___ 7. do homework

3. Read about Nora Lim. Complete the story. Use the words in the boxes.

eats	gets up	~~relaxes~~	takes

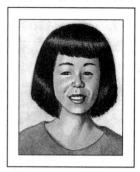

Nora Lim has a busy week. Sundays are busy, too, but she

_____relaxes_____ a little more. She _____ at
　　　　a.　　　　　　　　　　　　　　　　　　b.

8:00 and _____ a long, hot shower. Then
　　　　　　　　c.

she _____ breakfast with her family.
　　　　　d.

drives	goes	leaves	makes	picks up

After breakfast she _____ her husband to the shoe store. Then she
　　　　　　　　　　　　　e.

takes the children to their Aunt Ellen. Ellen _____ lunch for them.
　　　　　　　　　　　　　　　　　　　　　　　　　f.

After lunch, Nora _____ Ellen's house and _____ to
　　　　　　　　　　　g.　　　　　　　　　　　　　　　　　　h.

the library for two hours. At 4:00 she _____ the children from Ellen's.
　　　　　　　　　　　　　　　　　　　　　i.

eats	gets	goes	makes	takes	watches

Nora _____ home at 5:00 and _____ dinner. Her
　　　　j.　　　　　　　　　　　　　　　　　k.

daughter, Sara, helps her. Dan _____ the bus home. The family
　　　　　　　　　　　　　　　　l.

_____ dinner at 6:00. They talk about their day. After dinner, Nora
　　m.

_____ TV with her family. At 10:00 Nora _____ to bed.
　n.　　　　　　　　　　　　　　　　　　　　　　　　　　o.

4. What about you? Complete your weekday or weekend schedule. Use your own paper. Use the schedule in Exercise 1 as an example.

Challenge Interview someone you know (a friend, family member, or classmate). Write a schedule of his or her daily routine.

Life Events

1. Look in your dictionary. Complete the timeline for Martin Perez.

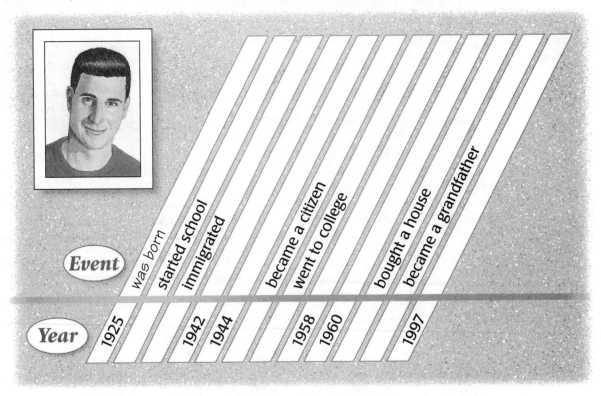

Event	was born	started school	immigrated		became a citizen	went to college		bought a house	became a grandfather	
Year	1925		1942	1944		1958	1960			1997

2. Complete the story about Rosa Lopez. Use the words in the box.

~~was~~	died	fell	got	got
graduated	had	learned	moved	rented

Rosa Lopez _____was_____ born in Canada
              a.

in 1928. She _____ from high school in 1945.
              b.

In 1946 she _____ to drive and
              c.

_____ to British Columbia. She _____
     d.   **e.**

a job and _____ an apartment with a friend.
              f.

Then she met Martin. They _____ in love, _____
              g.   **h.**

married, and _____ two children. They were very happy until Martin
              i.

_____ in 1997. Today Rosa lives in New Brunswick with her daughter and
     j.

grandchildren.

3. Match the words with the pictures. Write the number.

_4_ a. **Now you can drive!**

___ b. **This number is important!**

___ c. **You are now husband and wife.**

___ d. **Congratulations! Are you going to go to college now?**

___ e. **Now you can travel to Spain, China, Egypt,...**

1.

OFFICE OF THE CITY CLERK   № 18525
MARRIAGE LICENCE BUREAU
Certificate of Marriage Registration
This Is To Certify That ___Daniel Edward Gutman___
and ___Nina Wallace___
Were Married
on ___September 25, 1998___
at ___Winnipeg, Manitoba___   ___October 20, 1998___
CERTIFIED THIS DATE

2.

CANADA
PASSPORT / PASSEPORT   CANADA
P   CAN   SH159172
PEREZ
MARTIN
CANADIAN/CANADIEN
TORONTO

3.

Employment and   Emploi et
Immigration Canada   Immigration Canada
SOCIAL   NUMÉRO
INSURANCE   D'ASSURANCE
NUMBER   SOCIALE
476 012 000
MARTIN PEREZ
SIGNATURE   Martin Perez

4.

Ontario   Driver's Licence
                 Permis de conduire
NUMBER/NUMÉRO
S1567-56205-86106
PEREZ,
MARTIN
G
CANADA

5.

Halifax High School
Daniel Gutman
June 1994
David Glaser
Jean Horn

4. What about you? Check (✔) the documents you have.

☐ birth certificate   ☐ Social Insurance card
☐ high school diploma   ☐ driver's licence
☐ college diploma/university degree   ☐ passport

Challenge Look at **page 183** in this book. Complete the timeline.

Feelings

1. Look in your dictionary. Write all the words that end in *-y* and *-ed*.

-Y	-ED	
thirsty	disgusted	
___	___	___
___	___	___
___	___	___
___	___	___
___	___	

2. How do these people feel? Use words from Exercise 1.

a. ___relieved___   b. ___   c. ___

d. ___   e. ___

f. ___   g. ___   h. ___

i. ___   j. ___

3. Put these words in the correct columns.

~~bored~~	~~calm~~	comfortable	homesick	full	in love
in pain	**nervous**	**proud**	**uncomfortable**	**sick**	**well**

🙂		🙁	
calm	_____	_bored_	_____
_____	_____	_____	_____
_____	_____	_____	_____

4. Complete the conversations. Use words from Exercise 3.

a. **Are you hot? cold?**   No. I'm _comfortable_ , thanks.

b. **So, do you like Sandy?**   *Like?* I'm _____!

c. **What's wrong?**   Oh, I'm _____. I miss my family, my friends, my country…

d. **Wow! Your son got 100%!**   Yes. I'm very _____ of him.

e. **What's wrong?**   I'm _____. Please call a doctor.

f. **Is today your English test?**   Yes. I'm very _____.

5. What about you? How do you feel when you…? Circle as many words as possible for each question. Add new words too.

a. **wake up**	sleepy	happy	calm	_____
b. **start a new class**	nervous	confused	excited	_____
c. **have problems in school**	worried	upset	homesick	_____
d. **talk with your boss**	happy	nervous	comfortable	_____
e. _____	_____	_____	_____	_____

Challenge   Look at **page 183** in this book. Answer the question.

A Graduation

1. Look in your dictionary. **True** or **False**?

    a. A graduate is crying.   _____False_____

    b. The valedictorian is on the stage.   _____

    c. The guest speaker is wearing a cap and gown.   _____

    d. The photographer is taking a picture of the audience.   _____

2. Match the photos with the captions. Write the letter.

   _e_ **1.** This is Mom crying.

   ___ **4.** Miguel is giving his speech.

   ___ **2.** Here's Dad taking a picture.

   ___ **3.** The podium

   ___ **5.** Grandma is applauding.

   ___ **6.** The audience

   ___ **7.** The proud graduates

   ___ **8.** Miguel is getting his diploma.

3. Look at page 33 in your dictionary. Which invitation goes with the picture? Circle the letter.

You Are Invited to a Party

Bring a Guest!

Music! Dancing! Buffet!

a.

An Invitation

WHAT: Graduation Party

WHEN: Friday, June 11
1:00 P.M.

WHERE: 25 Grove St.

OUTDOOR BUFFET
MUSIC & DANCING

b.

It's a Graduation Party!

Please come on Friday,
June 11, at 1:00 P.M.

JOHN'S PIZZERIA

NO GIFTS PLEASE!!!

c.

4. Look at the picture. Circle the correct words to complete the sentences.

   a. This is a graduation ceremony /(party.)

   b. Two guests are hugging / kissing.

   c. There are four guests / gifts on the dance floor.

   d. A guest / caterer is toasting the graduates.

   e. A DJ / caterer is laughing.

   f. There's a beautiful banner / buffet in the picture.

5. What about you? Circle all the things you like at parties.

   a buffet   a DJ   gifts   a dance floor   Other: _____

Challenge Imagine you are having a graduation party. Design an invitation.

▶ **Go to page 171 for Another Look (Unit 2).**

Places to Live

1. Look in your dictionary. Where are they?

    a. students   _university residence_

    b. an elderly, physically-challenged woman   _____

    c. a man with a newspaper   _____

2. Look at the chart. Circle the correct words to complete the statements.

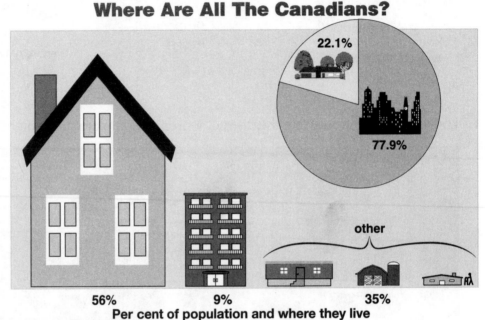

Where Are All The Canadians?

22.1%

77.9%

56%   9%   other   35%

Per cent of population and where they live

Statistics Canada: Catalogues 93-357-XPB, 93F0022XDB96012, and 93F0022XDB96013

    a. Most people live in the (city) / country.

    b. Only 22% of the people live in the <u>city / country</u>.

    c. Most people live in <u>houses / apartment buildings</u>.

    d. About <u>35% / 9%</u> of the people live in places which are not apartments or houses.

    e. Almost 80% of the population lives in the <u>city / country</u>.

3. What about you? Check (✓) the places where you've lived.

☐ city   ☐ suburbs   ☐ small town

☐ country   ☐ farm   ☐ ranch

☐ apartment building   ☐ house   ☐ semi-detached house

☐ university residence   ☐ townhouse   ☐ Other: _____

Challenge   Take a class survey. Where do your classmates live? Write the results.

                   Example: *Five students live in apartments,…*

1. Look in your dictionary. Circle the correct words to complete the sentences.

   a. The woman in A wants to <u>buy</u> /(rent) an apartment.

   b. She talks to the <u>manager / Realtor</u>.

   c. The rent is <u>$450 / $1100</u>.

   d. The man and woman in G are looking for a new <u>apartment / house</u>.

   e. The <u>Realtor makes / man and woman make</u> an offer.

   f. The <u>rent / mortgage</u> is $1100.

2. Check (✔) the things you have to do to rent an apartment and/or buy a house.

	RENT AN APARTMENT	BUY A HOUSE
a. talk to the manager	✔	☐
b. make an offer	☐	☐
c. sign a lease	☐	☐
d. get a loan	☐	☐
e. take ownership	☐	☐
f. move in	☐	☐
g. pay the rent	☐	☐
h. pay the mortgage	☐	☐
i. unpack	☐	☐
j. arrange the furniture	☐	☐

3. What about you? Check (✔) the things you and your family have done in the last ten years.

☐ looked for a new apartment   ☐ made an offer

☐ looked for a new house   ☐ gotten a loan

☐ signed a rental agreement   ☐ paid a mortgage

☐ paid rent   ☐ talked to a manager

☐ talked to a Realtor   ☐ moved

Challenge How did you find your home? Write a paragraph.

Apartments

1. Look in your dictionary. Who said...?

a.   **Good morning, Mrs. Cooper.**   _____doorman_____

b.   **When can I get the keys to my apartment?**   _____

c.   **Here's your lease. Please sign it here.**   _____

d.   **There's a vacancy in Apartment 3.**   _____

e.   **Hi, Jane. Thanks for getting my mail last week.**   _____

2. Look at the notice. **True** or **False**?

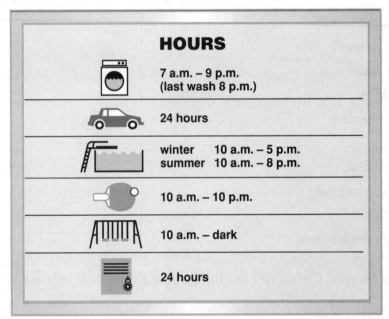

HOURS

🧺	7 a.m. – 9 p.m. (last wash 8 p.m.)
🚗	24 hours
🏊	winter 10 a.m. – 5 p.m. summer 10 a.m. – 8 p.m.
🏓	10 a.m. – 10 p.m.
🛝	10 a.m. – dark
🔒	24 hours

a. The swimming pool is always open until 8:00 P.M.   _____False_____

b. You can use the laundry room all night.   _____

c. The garage is always open.   _____

d. The playground always closes at 7:00 P.M.   _____

e. You can use the storage lockers at midnight.   _____

f. The rec room is open 24 hours.   _____

3. Circle the correct words to complete these notices.

a.
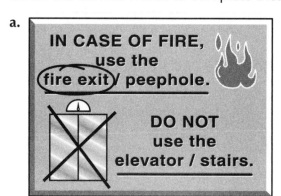
IN CASE OF FIRE, use the (fire exit) / peephole.

DO NOT use the elevator / stairs.

b.
NEW TENANTS: Please put your name on your balcony / mailbox.

c.
NOTICE
Do not throw...

Hangers   Aerosol cans

Glass bottles or jars   Newspapers

...down the garbage chute/garbage can.

d.
ATTENTION ALL TENANTS: Do not allow strangers into the building. Always use the intercom / doorknob.

4. What about you? Does your home have a(n)...? Check (✓) **Yes** or **No**.

	YES	NO	IF YES, WHERE?
a. fire escape	☐	☐	_____
b. security system	☐	☐	_____
c. laundry room	☐	☐	_____
d. garage	☐	☐	_____
e. balcony	☐	☐	_____
f. air conditioner	☐	☐	_____
g. smoke detector	☐	☐	_____
h. lobby	☐	☐	_____
i. security gate	☐	☐	_____

Challenge   Look at apartment ads in the newspaper. What do the apartments have? Use your dictionary for help. **Example:** *This apartment has an air conditioner...*

A House

1. Look in your dictionary. **Open** or **Closed**?

   a. front door   <u> Closed </u>   **d.** mailbox   <u>   </u>

   b. shutters   <u>   </u>   **e.** screen door   <u>   </u>

   c. storm door   <u>   </u>   **f.** windows   <u>   </u>

2. Look at this house. **True** or **False**?

   a. This is a <u>two-storey</u> house.   <u> False </u>

   b. The house has a <u>grey</u> garage door.   <u>   </u>

   c. The doorbell is to the <u>right</u> of the front door. <u>   </u>

   d. There is a chair on the <u>front walk</u>.   <u>   </u>

   e. The TV antenna is <u>in the front yard</u>.   <u>   </u>

   f. The chimney is <u>on the roof</u>.   <u>   </u>

   g. The fence is in the <u>backyard</u>.   <u>   </u>

3. What about you? Would you like to live in this house? Check (✔) **Yes** or **No**.

   ☐ Yes   ☐ No   Why? _____

Challenge Look at Exercise 2. Change the <u>underlined</u> words in the false sentences. Make the sentences true.

1. Look in your dictionary. Where's the…? Use the words in the box.

on the lawn	on the patio

a. garbage can   <u>on the patio</u>   **d.** furniture   _____

b. hammock   _____   **e.** sprinkler   _____

c. compost pile   _____   **f.** barbecue   _____

2. Put these words in the correct column.

~~bush~~   flower   flowerpot   garbage can   hedge   lawn
pruning shears   rake   shovel   trowel   watering can   wheelbarrow

GARDEN TOOLS	VEGETATION	CONTAINERS
_____	<u>bush</u>	_____
_____	_____	_____
_____	_____	_____
_____	_____	_____

3. Look at the garden and the list. Check (✔) the <u>completed</u> jobs.

Great Gardens
LANDSCAPERS

☑ water the plants

❏ weed the flower bed

❏ mow the lawn

❏ plant trees

❏ trim the hedge

❏ rake the leaves

Challenge Look at the yard in your dictionary. What would you like to do there? Write a few sentences. Begin with *I'd like…*. **Example:** *I'd like to sit on the patio.*

A Kitchen

1. Look in your dictionary. Where can you find the…? Use the words in the box.

on	under

a. paper towels <u>under the cabinet</u>   **d.** pot   _____

b. dish drainer   _____   **e.** oven drawer   _____

c. bread   _____   **f.** garburator   _____

2. Look at the bar graph. Put the words in the correct column.

Based on information from: Shook, M. and R.: *It's About Time!* (NY: Penguin Books, 1992)

THINGS THAT LAST 10 YEARS		THINGS THAT LAST 15 YEARS
___<u>blender</u>___	_____	_____
_____	_____	_____
_____	_____	

3. What about you? Check (✔) the appliances you have. Answer the questions.

	WHERE IS IT?	HOW LONG HAVE YOU HAD IT?
☐ blender	_____	_____
☐ toaster oven	_____	_____
☐ coffee maker	_____	_____
☐ mixer	_____	_____
☐ refrigerator	_____	_____
☐ microwave	_____	_____
☐ Other: _____	_____	_____

Challenge Look at the kitchen appliances in your dictionary. List the five you think are the most important. Compare your list with a classmate's list.

1. Look in your dictionary. **True** or **False**?

   a. The set of dishes is blue, white, and pink.   _____True_____

   b. There's a teapot on the tray.   _____

   c. The ceiling fan has two light fixtures.   _____

   d. The tablecloth is white.   _____

   e. There's a vase in the china cabinet.   _____

   f. The salt shaker is to the left of the pepper shaker.   _____

   g. There's a mug on the dining room table.   _____

2. Look at this table setting. Complete the sentences.

   a. The _____bowl_____ is for soup.

   b. The _____ is under the bowl.

   c. The plate and bowl are on top of the _____.

   d. There are two _____ to the left of the plate.

   e. They aren't on the folded _____. They're next to it.

   f. There are two _____. They're to the right of the plate.

   g. There's also a _____ to the right of the plate.

   h. There's a _____. It's for water.

3. What about you? How does your table setting look? Draw a picture on your own paper. Then complete the chart.

ITEM	HOW MANY?	WHERE?
knife		
fork		
spoon		
plate		
bowl		

ITEM	HOW MANY?	WHERE?
glass		
placemat		
napkin		
Other: _____		
_____		

Challenge   Tell a classmate how to draw the place setting from your table. Does it look the same as your picture in Exercise 3?

A Living Room

1. Look in your dictionary. How many … are there?

   a. throw pillows __3__ **b.** logs _____ **c.** baskets _____

   d. paintings _____ **e.** lightbulbs in the track lighting _____

2. Look at the Millers' new living room. Cross out the items they have <u>already</u> bought.

TO BUY

~~couch~~   carpet
love seat   track lighting
armchair   floor lamp
colour TV   plant
stereo   magazine holder
wall unit   drapes
bookcase   fire screen
coffee table   logs
throw pillows   end table

3. What about you? Look at the checklist in Exercise 2. List the items you have. Use your own paper.

Challenge Write six sentences about the Millers' living room. **Example:** *They have a couch, but they don't have a love seat.*

1. Look in your dictionary. Where are they? Check (✔) the correct columns.

	SINK	BATHTUB/SHOWER	WALL	FLOOR
a. towel racks		✔	✔	
b. hot water				
c. faucets				
d. tiles				
e. mats				
f. drains				
g. toothbrush holder				

2. Look at the ad. Circle the correct words to complete the sentences.

a. The (bath mat) / rubber mat is $9.99. **e.** The toilet brush / toothbrush is $4.99.

b. The hamper / wastebasket is $6.99. **f.** The toilet paper / washcloth is $3.99.

c. The bath towel / hand towel is $5.99. **g.** The towel rack / scale is $27.99.

d. The soap dish / soap is $2.99.

Challenge Look at an ad or in a store. What do these items cost?

a toothbrush _____   a wastebasket _____

a soap dish _____   a bath mat _____

A Bedroom

1. Look in your dictionary. What colour is the…?

a. bedspread ___purple___ **b.** mattress _____ **c.** lamp _____

2. Cross out the word that doesn't belong.

a. They're electric.	~~mirror~~	outlet	light switch	clock radio
b. They're soft.	pillowcase	dust ruffle	headboard	blanket
c. They're part of a bed.	mattress	lamp	box spring	bed frame
d. They're on the floor.	bed frame	lampshade	rug	night table
e. They make the room dark.	lampshade	curtains	window shade	dresser
f. You put things in them.	closet	drawer	photographs	night table

3. Complete the conversations. Use words from Exercise 2.

a. Lee: What time is it?

   Mom: I don't know. There's a ___clock radio___ on the night table.

b. Tom: I'm cold.

   Ana: Here's an extra _____.

c. Ray: The bed's uncomfortable.

   Mia: The _____ is too soft.

d. Amir: There's no window shade.

   Marwa: Close the _____.

e. Bill: My sweater's not in the drawer.

   Molly: Look in the _____.

4. What about you? Check (✓) the items that are on your bed.

☐ fitted sheet   Colour: _____

☐ flat sheet   Colour: _____

☐ bedspread   Colour: _____

☐ pillow(s)   How many? _____   Hard or soft? _____

☐ mattress   Hard or soft? _____

☐ blankets   How many? _____

☐ Other: _____

Challenge   Write a paragraph describing your bedroom.

44

1. Look in your dictionary. Which four items are for safety?

a. ___night light___   c. _____

b. _____   d. _____

2. Look at Sue and Mindy's room. There are 12 dolls in the room. Find and circle them.

Write the locations of the dolls. Use your own paper. Use *on, under,* and *in.*

Example: *under the bunk bed*

3. What about you? Check (✔) the things you played with when you were a child.

☐ dolls   ☐ teddy bears   ☐ crayons   ☐ puzzles

☐ stuffed animals ☐ balls   ☐ Other: _____

Challenge Look at the toys you checked in Exercise 3. Write a paragraph about your favourite one.

Housework

1. Look in your dictionary. What are the people doing? Use the *-ing* form of the verb.

   a. **Can we do this with magazines, too?** <u>recycling the newspapers</u>

   b. **Dad, does this teddy bear go here?** _____

   c. **I like this new bedspread.** _____

   d. **Is this the last plate, Dad?** _____

2. Look at the room. What housework did Todd do? Check (✓) the <u>completed</u> jobs.

To Do
☑ wash the sheets
☐ change the sheets
☐ sweep the floor
☐ empty the wastebasket
☐ dust the dresser
☐ clean the sink
☐ mop the bathroom floor
☐ take out the newspapers

3. What about you? How often do you…? Check (✓) the correct column.

	ALWAYS	SOMETIMES	NEVER
dust the furniture			
polish the furniture			
recycle the newspapers			
wash the dishes			
vacuum the carpet			
wipe the counter			
scrub the floor			
put away clothes			
Other: _____			

Challenge Write a *To Do* list of housework for this week.

1. Look in your dictionary. What can you use to clean the...?

WINDOWS	FLOOR	DISHES
glass cleaner	_____	_____
_____	_____	_____
	_____	_____

2. Match each item with the correct coupon. Write the letter.

To Buy:

_d_ 1. feather duster

____ 2. steel-wool pads

____ 3. sponges

____ 4. pail

____ 5. cleanser

____ 6. garbage bags

____ 7. dishwashing liquid

____ 8. rubber gloves

____ 9. vacuum cleaner bags

a. Lenny's COUPON **$2.99** 51 cm x 56 cm Strongy — Limit 3 Pks. Expires 2-3-03

b. Lenny's COUPON **$1.89** 950 mL — Limit 3 Expires 2-3-03

c. Lenny's COUPON **$1.99** 8 L — Limit 2 Expires 2-3-03

d. Lenny's COUPON **$1.99** — Limit 2 Expires 2-3-03

e. Lenny's COUPON Cleanest 3/ **$1.00** — Limit 6 Expires 2-3-03

f. Lenny's COUPON **99¢/ pair** — Limit 4 prs. Expires 2-3-03

g. Lenny's COUPON **$1.99/ pk of 12** — Limit 3 pks Expires 2-3-99

h. Lenny's COUPON **$1.59** — Limit 2 Expires 2-3-03

i. Lenny's COUPON **2-pack $3.19** — Limit 2 Expires 2-3-03

3. What about you? Look at the cleaning supplies in Exercise 2. Which ones do you have? What do you use them for? Make a list on your own paper.

Example: *feather duster—dust the desk*

Challenge Look in a store or at newspaper ads. Write the prices of some cleaning supplies that you use.

Household Problems and Repairs

1. Look in your dictionary. Who said…?

a. [I'm up on the roof.] ____roofer____

b. [Good-bye termites!] _____

c. [I'm turning the power on again.] _____

d. [I'll fix the toilet next.] _____

e. [I'm fixing the lock on the front door.] _____

f. [I have one more step to do.] _____

g. [I'm putting in new windows.] _____

2. Look at John's bathroom. There are seven problems. Find and circle them.

True or **False**? Change the <u>underlined</u> words in the false sentences. Make the sentences true.

a. The <u>sink</u> tap is dripping.   ____False. The bathtub tap is dripping.____

b. The <u>window</u> is broken.   _____

c. There are <u>ants</u> near the sink.   _____

d. The <u>light</u> isn't working.   _____

e. The <u>sink</u> is overflowing.   _____

f. The <u>mirror</u> is cracked.   _____

3. Look at the picture in Exercise 2 and these ads. Who should John call? Complete his list. Include the company name, the phone number, and the problem(s). (*Hint:* John will use some of the companies for more than one problem.)

224   YELLOW PAGES

ABC ELECTRIC CORP.
• Licensed Electricians
• Free Estimates
555-2656

Free estimates
HAMPTON CARPENTERS INC.
• closets   • wall units
• shelves   • shutters
• cabinets • bookcases
555-7367

JACK O. TRADES
GENERAL REPAIRS
No job is too small.
555-8356

Keys Made While-U-Wait
UNIVERSITY LOCKSMITHS
Your one-stop security shop
555-9946

EXTERMINALL PEST CONTROL
Fast and Safe
Residential and Commercial
555-4789

Affordable Home Remodelling
HARMON ROOFING REPAIRS
• *All types of roofing*
• *leaders & gutters*
• *Licensed & Insured*
555-7587
"We care about yo...

Tell the Advertisers you found them in the **Yellow Pages**

EMERGENCY SERVICES
24 HOURS
7 DAYS A WEEK
Free Flow Plumbing Co.
555-2233

Let your fing...
the walking i...
Yellow Pa...

Why wonder...
buy it?
The **Yellow**
tell you *wher...*

Call
1. exterminator _____ 555-4789
   a. cockroaches
2. _____ _____
   a. dripping tap
   b.
   c.
3. _____ _____
   a.
4. _____ _____
   a.
   b.

Challenge   Look at the problems in Exercise 3. Who fixes them in your home? Make a list. Use the phone book if necessary. **Example:** *broken window—my cousin Paul*

▶ **Go to page 172 for Another Look (Unit 3).**

49

Fruit

1. Look in your dictionary. Write the name of the fruit.

   a. They're to the left of the pears.   <u>peaches</u>

   b. They're below the apricots.   _____

   c. They're above the nuts.   _____

   d. They're to the right of the cantaloupes. _____ and _____

   e. They're to the right of the raspberries and blueberries. _____

   f. One of them is over ripe.   _____

2. Complete the ad. Use the words in the box.

apples	avocados	grapefruit	grapes	lemons	limes
oranges	pears	~~pineapples~~	strawberries		

Fresh Fruit Values

Fresh Hawaiian <u>pineapples</u> Only $2.99

California Haas — Great for Guacamole — 99¢ each

Chilean Imported Bartlett — $1.29/lb $2.84/kg

Juicy Florida — $2.49 / 1.36 kg bag

Pink — 4 / $1.00

Your Choice ___ or ___ — 4 / $1.00

Sweet Ripe — $3.89 / box

Crisp Granny Smith — $2.49/1.36 kg bag

Large Bunch Seedless — $3.99/lb $8.80/kg

3. What about you? Look at the fruits in Exercise 2. Make a shopping list. Use your own paper. What will you buy? How much or how many? How much will it cost?

   Example: *2 avocados—$1.98*

Challenge Make a list of fruit from your country.

1. Look in your dictionary. Which vegetables are...? Put them in the correct column.

YELLOW/ORANGE	GREEN		RED
carrots			

2. Look at the chart.

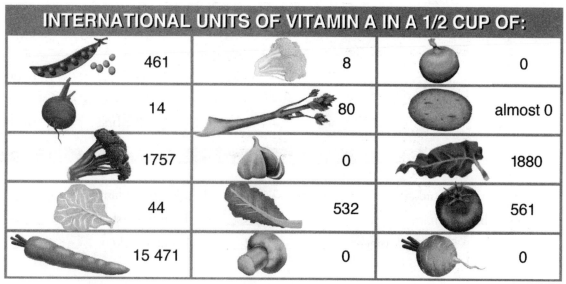

INTERNATIONAL UNITS OF VITAMIN A IN A 1/2 CUP OF:		
461	8	0
14	80	almost 0
1757	0	1880
44	532	561
15 471	0	0

Based on information from: Netzer, C.: *The Encyclopedia of Food Values.* (NY: Dell Publishing, 1992)

Which has more vitamin A? Circle the correct answer.

a. lettuce / spinach   **d.** carrots / celery

b. broccoli / cauliflower   **e.** potatoes / tomatoes

c. beets / turnips   **f.** cabbage / lettuce

3. What about you? How often do you eat these vegetables? Circle the numbers.

CARROTS	0	1	2	3	4	4+	TIMES A WEEK
BROCCOLI	0	1	2	3	4	4+	TIMES A WEEK
SPINACH	0	1	2	3	4	4+	TIMES A WEEK
TOMATOES	0	1	2	3	4	4+	TIMES A WEEK

Challenge Make a list of vegetables from your country.

Meat and Poultry

1. Look in your dictionary. Which meats have bones? Which meats don't have bones? Make a list on your own paper.

    Example: *with bones—steak*   *boneless—roast beef*

2. Look at the chart. Write the cooking times. Use numbers.

	SIZE	COOKING TIME	METHOD
	4 cm or 1½" thick	10 min.*	broiler
	1.5 cm or ½" thick	3 min.*	broiler
	2–4 kg	60 min. per kg	oven
	3–9 kg	45 min. per kg	oven
	3–5 kg	3–4 hrs.	oven
	1–2 kg	1½ hrs.	oven

*each side

a. 4 kg turkey   <u>3–4 hours</u>   d. 3 kg leg of lamb _____

b. 4 kg ham   _____   e. 4 cm thick steak _____

c. 1.5 cm thick piece _____   f. 1.5 kg chicken   _____
   of liver

3. Label the chicken parts. Use the words in the box.

~~breast~~   drumstick   thigh   wing

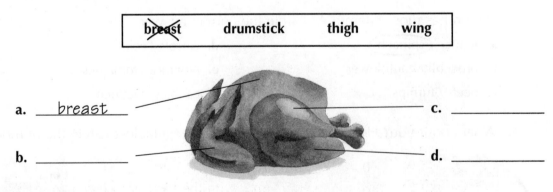

a. <u>breast</u>   c. _____

b. _____   d. _____

4. What about you? Check (✔) the meat and poultry you eat.

    ☐ veal cutlets   ☐ bacon   ☐ duck   ☐ gizzards   ☐ tripe

Challenge Take a survey. Ask five people which meats and poultry they eat.

52

1. Look in your dictionary. Write the names of the seafood.

a. <u>halibut</u>   d. _____   g. _____   j. _____

b. _____   e. _____   h. _____   k. _____

c. _____   f. _____   i. _____   l. _____

2. Look at the sandwich and the order form. Check (✔) the correct boxes.

Sandwich Order

Meat/Fish
- ☑ smoked turkey
- ☐ roast beef
- ☐ corned beef
- ☐ salami
- ☐ pastrami
- ☐ filet of sole

Cheese
- ☐ processed
- ☐ mozzarella
- ☐ Swiss
- ☐ cheddar

Bread
- ☐ white
- ☐ whole wheat
- ☐ rye

Side
- ☐ potato salad
- ☐ pasta salad
- ☐ coleslaw

3. What about you? Complete your order with the food from the form in Exercise 2.

A _____ sandwich on _____ bread with a side

of _____ .

Challenge Ask five classmates what they want from the deli. Write their orders.

The Supermarket

1. Look at the supermarket in your dictionary. Where are these items? Complete the chart.

	SECTION NAME	LOCATION
a. soup	canned goods	aisle 1B
b. chicken		
c. tomatoes		across from the dairy section
d. bread		
e. milk		behind the produce section
f. pop		to the left of the doors
g. ice cream		to the right of the produce section
h. flour		
i. toilet paper		
j. candy bars		near the checkout

2. Complete the conversations. Use the words in the box.

Bagger	bottle return	cart	Cashier
checkouts	~~Manager~~	plastic	

Amy: Excuse me. Where do I take these empty pop bottles?

__Manager__ : To the _____. Near aisle 1.
     a.   **b.**

Amy: I'll get a shopping basket.

Jason: Get a shopping _____! We have a lot on our list.
                    c.

Amy: Look at the _____!
                      d.

Jason: Oh, no. The lines are really long.

Jason: What's the total?

_____: $87.67
  e.

Amy: Can we have four bags?

_____: Sure. Paper or _____?
  f.   **g.**

3. Look at Amy and Jason's shopping list. Put the items in the correct category.

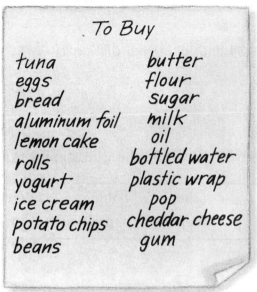

To Buy

tuna   butter
eggs   flour
bread   sugar
aluminum foil milk
lemon cake   oil
rolls   bottled water
yogurt   plastic wrap
ice cream   pop
potato chips cheddar cheese
beans   gum

CANNED GOODS	FROZEN FOODS	BAKING PRODUCTS	DAIRY SECTION
tuna	_____	_____	_____
_____		_____	_____
		_____	_____
			_____
			_____

BEVERAGES	PAPER PRODUCTS	BAKED GOODS	SNACK FOODS
_____	_____	_____	_____
_____	_____	_____	_____
		_____	

4. Look at the things Amy and Jason bought. Cross the items off the shopping list in Exercise 3.

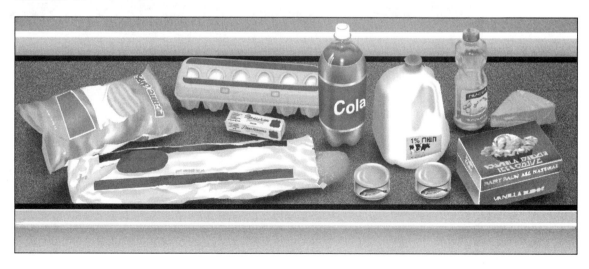

Challenge Make a shopping list. Write the section for each item. **Example:** *scallops—fish section*

Containers and Packaged Foods

1. Look at **pages 54 and 55** in your dictionary. Write the container or package for these items.

   a. beans   <u> can </u>   **c.** instant coffee   _____

   b. cake mix   _____   **d.** margarine   _____

2. Complete these coupons. Use the words in the box.

bag	bottle	carton	loaf
six-pack	package	roll	~~tube~~

BRIGHT'S

Bright's Toothpaste

2/$1

75 mL <u>tube</u>

LIMIT 2

a.

SPECIAL!

2 L Orange Juice

$1.50/

b.

SAVE 50¢

Cola

one
Regular or Diet

c.

BUY ONE GET ONE **FREE**

Maine Spring Water

500 mL

d.

BUY ONE GET ONE **FREE**

SMARTS

SMART'S POTATO CHIPS
low salt

LIMIT 1 FREE ITEM

250 g

e.

Stop and Save

RYE BREAD

99¢

Limit 1 per customer

675 g

f.

SPECIAL!

Chip's Cookies
all varieties

350 g

$1.99

Chips!

g.

100 sheets

Strongy Paper Towels

3/$2

h.

3. Tiffany used all the coupons in Exercise 2. Write her shopping list. Use your own paper.

   Example: *2 tubes of toothpaste*

_____ **Challenge** Which foods do you <u>think</u> are in your refrigerator? Make a list. Then check your answers at home. Include the foods and their containers. **Example:** *a bottle of pop*

1. Look in your dictionary. Match the abbreviations with the words. Write the number.

<u>2</u> **a.** mL

___ **b.** kg

___ **c.** L

___ **d.** g

___ **e.** c.

___ **f.** tsp.

___ **g.** TBS.

1. teaspoon

2. millilitre

3. kilogram

4. gram

5. cup

6. tablespoon

7. litre

2. Write the weight or measurement. Use the complete word, not the abbreviation.

a. <u>1.5 kilograms of potatoes</u>

b. _____

c. _____

d. _____

e. _____

f. _____

Challenge Look at **page 183** in this book. Follow the instructions.

Food Preparation

1. Look in your dictionary. Read the recipe. <u>Underline</u> all the food preparation words.

Baked Carrots

450 g or 1 lb. carrots   5 mL or 1 tsp. sugar
45 mL or 3 TBS. butter   120 mL or ½ cup water
1 small onion
salt, pepper, nutmeg

Chop the onion. Peel and grate the
carrots. Grease a small pan.

(continued)
Add the onion and cook until soft. Stir
in the carrots. Add the sugar, salt,
pepper, nutmeg, and water. Pour into a
covered casserole dish. Bake at
350°F (180°C) until soft, about 30–40
minutes.

2. Look at the recipe in Exercise 1. Number the pictures in order.

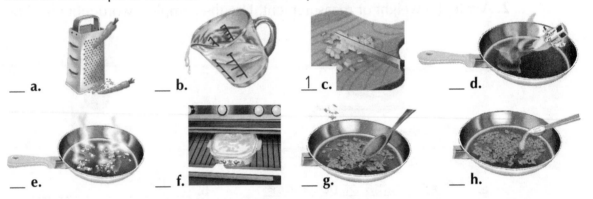

__ a.   __ b.   1 c.   __ d.

__ e.   __ f.   __ g.   __ h.

3. Look at the pictures. Circle the correct words to complete the recipe.

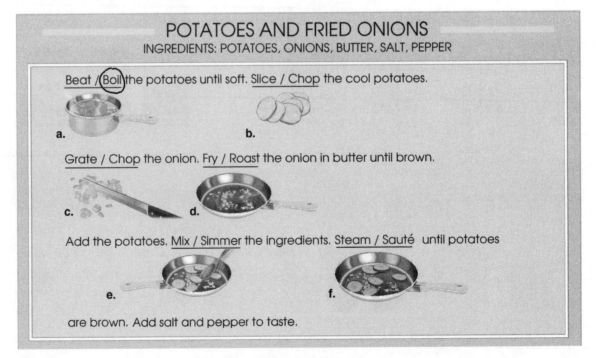

POTATOES AND FRIED ONIONS
INGREDIENTS: POTATOES, ONIONS, BUTTER, SALT, PEPPER

Beat / (Boil) the potatoes until soft. Slice / Chop the cool potatoes.

a.   b.

Grate / Chop the onion. Fry / Roast the onion in butter until brown.

c.   d.

Add the potatoes. Mix / Simmer the ingredients. Steam / Sauté until potatoes

e.   f.

are brown. Add salt and pepper to taste.

Challenge Write the recipe for one of your favourite foods. Share it with a classmate.

1. Look in your dictionary. **True** or **False**?

   a. The grater is below the steamer. _____False_____

   b. There's lettuce in the colander. _____

   c. The whisk and strainer are on the wall. _____

   d. The ladle is in the pot. _____

   e. The lid is on the double boiler. _____

   f. The spatula is above the tongs. _____

2. Match the words that go together. Write the number.

   _6_ **a.** cake   **1.** beater

   ___ **b.** mixing   **2.** opener

   ___ **c.** egg   **3.** boiler

   ___ **d.** garlic   **4.** sheet

   ___ **e.** double   **5.** holder

   ___ **f.** pot   **6.** pan

   ___ **g.** rolling   **7.** bowl

   ___ **h.** cookie   **8.** press

   ___ **i.** can   **9.** pin

3. Fill in the blanks. Use the words in Exercise 2.

SOME KITCHEN UTENSILS

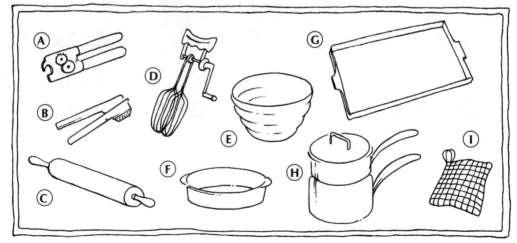

   a. _can opener_   **d.** _____   **g.** _____

   b. _____   **e.** _____   **h.** _____

   c. _____   **f.** _____   **i.** _____

Challenge List the five most important kitchen utensils. Why are they important?
Example: *pot—to cook spaghetti, soups, and vegetables*

1. Look in your dictionary. What can you eat or drink with…?

A STRAW	YOUR FINGERS	
pop		

2. Check (✔) the items that are on the hamburger.

Hamburger with:

☑ cheese   ☐ ketchup

☐ onions   ☐ mustard

☐ lettuce   ☐ mayonnaise

☐ tomato   ☐ relish

3. Look at the information. Number the items in order of their calories. (Number 1 has the most calories.)

67 Kj/16 cal.	63 Kj/15 cal.	424 Kj/101 cal.	63 Kj/15 cal.	193 Kj/46 cal.
___ sugar	_1_ mayonnaise	___ mustard/relish		___ ketchup

4. What about you? Check (✔) the condiments you use. What foods do you put them on?

CONDIMENT	FOODS
☐ ketchup	
☐ mustard	
☐ mayonnaise	
☐ relish	

Challenge   Find out how many kilojoules/calories are in some of your favourite fast foods.

1. Look in your dictionary. Complete the orders.

    a. Scrambled eggs, _____*sausage*_____, and _____.

    b. A _____ on whole wheat bread.

    c. _____, _____, and corn.

    d. _____ and bacon.

    e. Steak, a _____, and vegetables.

    f. Pasta and _____.

    g. Apple _____.

2. Look at the food. Complete the order.

FOOD ORDER

TABLE

roast chicken

GRATUITIES NOT INCLUDED   TOTAL

3. What about you? What's your favourite…?

    soup _____   dessert _____   hot beverage _____

Challenge Show five people the coffee shop menu in your dictionary. Write their orders.

1. Look in your dictionary. Who…?

    a. washes dishes   <u>dishwasher</u>

    b. leaves a tip   _____

    c. takes orders   _____

    d. cooks food   _____

    e. carries dessert trays   _____

    f. seats customers   _____

2. Look at the order and the place setting.

onion soup
house salad
steak
broccoli
mashed potatoes
garlic bread
half bottle of
    red wine
coffee

Check (✔) the items the place setting still needs.

☐ dinner plate	☐ wine glass	☐ dinner fork
✔ salad plate	☐ cup	☐ steak knife
☐ soup bowl	☐ saucer	☐ knife
☐ bread-and-butter plate	☐ napkin	☐ teaspoon
☐ water glass	☐ salad fork	☐ soup spoon

3. Look at the menu. Complete the bill.

Menu

Soup of the day $3.50
House salad 2.50

Fish of the day 15.50
Chicken l'orange 10.50
Sirloin steak 17.50

Vegetables 1.50
Potatoes 1.50

Cherry pie 3.50
with ice cream 4.00
Coconut cake 3.50

Coffee or tea 1.50

```
        The Bistro
      242 WEST STREET
        555-0700
        GUEST BILL

black bean soup              $3.50
house salad              _____
grilled salmon           _____
peas                     _____
french fries             _____
cherry pie w·vanilla ice cream _____
coffee                   _____
Subtotal                 _____
Tax(7%)                      $2.10
Total                    _____
        Thank you!
    Hope to see you again soon
```

4. In Canada, most restaurant patrons leave a tip. The tip is usually 15% of the subtotal. Look at the bill in Exercise 3. Complete the sentences with the correct answers.

a. The subtotal is ___$30.00___ . $30.00 $31.50 $36.22

b. A 15% tip is _____. $1.50 $4.50 $4.72

c. You should leave this tip on the _____.   menu   table   dessert tray

5. What about you? Do people leave tips for the server in your country? _____.
If yes, how much? _____ Where do they leave it? _____

Challenge Look at the menu in Exercise 3. Order a meal. Figure out the subtotal, 7% tax, the total, and a 15% tip.

▶ **Go to page 173 for Another Look (Unit 4).**

Clothing I

1. Look in your dictionary. What colour is/are the...?

   a. coveralls   _orange_   **d.** overalls   _____

   b. jeans   _____   **e.** sweatpants   _____

   c. cardigan   _____   **f.** jumper   _____

2. Which clothes do women usually wear? Men? Both women and men? Put the words from the box in the correct space.

~~blouse~~	dress	evening gown	jeans	jumper	leggings
maternity dress	pants	skirt	sports coat	sports shirt	suit	sweater
three-piece suit	tunic	T-shirt	turtleneck	tuxedo	uniform	vest

   Women Only

   blouse

   _____

   _____

   _____

   _____

   _____

   _____

   Women and Men

   _____

   _____

   _____

   _____

   _____

   _____

   _____

   Men Only

   _____

   _____

   _____

   _____

3. Put the names of the clothing items on the list.

To Pack for Chicago

a. _blue jeans_ and _white T-shirt_

b._____

c._____

d._____

e._____ and _____

4. Match the activity with the clothes from Exercise 3. Write the letter.

The Parkview Hotel

Saturday

_e_ 1. Meet Jane in exercise room—7:30 A.M.

____ 2. Meeting in Conference Room 23—9:00 A.M.–3:00 P.M.

____ 3. Relax in hotel room—3:00 P.M.–5:30 P.M.

____ 4. Dinner at The Grille with Greg Haines—6:30 P.M.

____ 5. Dance party at the Grand Hotel Ballroom—9:00 P.M.

5. What about you? When do you wear these clothes? Check (✔) the correct columns.

	AT SCHOOL	AT WORK	AT HOME	AT A PARTY	NEVER
suit					
jeans					
shorts					
sweatshirt and pants					
tuxedo or gown					
uniform					
Other: _____					

Challenge Look at the clothes in your dictionary. List eight items you have. When do you wear them?
Example: *dress—I wear it at work.*

Clothing II

1. Look in your dictionary. **True** or **False**?

   a. The man with the grey cap is wearing a jacket. _____True_____

   b. The woman with the toque is wearing green tights. _____

   c. The woman in the poncho is wearing yellow rainboots. _____

   d. The man with the baseball cap is wearing sunglasses. _____

2. Circle the correct words to complete the ad.

Dress for the Snow

Jessica is wearing a dark <u>down vest</u> /(parka,)
                                          a.
<u>toque / ski mask</u>, and <u>gloves / mittens</u>.
       b.   **c.**
Justin is wearing a black leather <u>coat / jacket</u>,
                                              d.
<u>earmuffs / hat</u>, and a <u>scarf / poncho</u>.
       e.   **f.**

Dress for the Sun

Kimberly is wearing a <u>baseball cap / straw hat</u>,
                                      g.
<u>swimming trunks / swimsuit</u>, and
          h.
a white <u>cover-up / windbreaker</u>. Her
               i.
<u>raincoat / umbrella</u> and <u>cap / sunglasses</u>
       j.   **k.**
protect her from the sun.

3. What about you? Circle the correct words to complete the statements.

   a. I <u>am / am not</u> wearing a jacket or coat today.

   b. I <u>wear / don't wear</u> sunglasses.

   c. I <u>sometimes / never</u> wear a hat.

Challenge Find pictures of people in a newspaper, magazine, or your dictionary. Describe their clothes. **Example:** *She's wearing a dark blue skirt, a white pullover,…*

1. Look in your dictionary. What colour is/are the...?

a. bike shorts   <u>black</u>   **e.** leotard   _____

b. slippers   _____   **f.** nightgown   _____

c. half slip   _____   **g.** kneesocks   _____

d. long underwear   _____   **h.** bathrobe   _____

2. Look at the ad. Complete the bill.

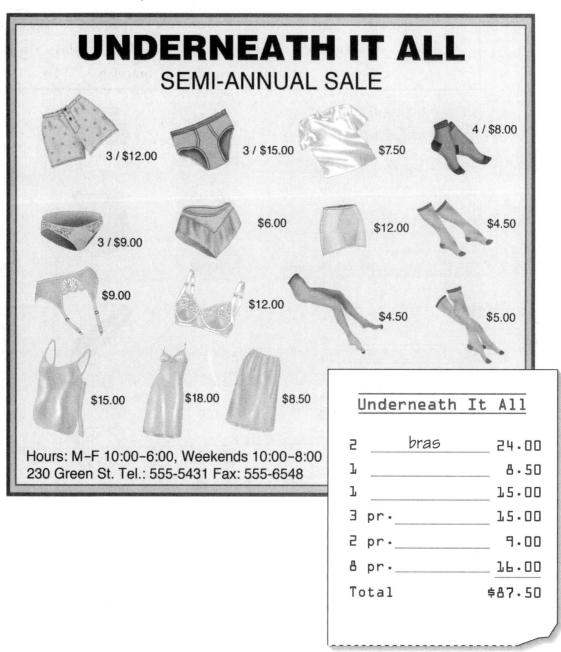

UNDERNEATH IT ALL
SEMI-ANNUAL SALE

3 / $12.00
3 / $15.00
$7.50
4 / $8.00

3 / $9.00
$6.00
$12.00
$4.50

$9.00
$12.00
$4.50
$5.00

$15.00
$18.00
$8.50

Hours: M–F 10:00–6:00, Weekends 10:00–8:00
230 Green St. Tel.: 555-5431 Fax: 555-6548

	Underneath It All	
2	bras	24.00
1	_____	8.50
1	_____	15.00
3 pr.	_____	15.00
2 pr.	_____	9.00
8 pr.	_____	16.00
Total		$87.50

Challenge   Choose clothes from the ad in Exercise 2. Write a bill. Figure out the total.

Shoes and Accessories

1. Look in your dictionary. How many … can you see?

a. sales clerks ____2____   **d.** bow ties in the case _____

b. people in line _____   **e.** handbags on the case _____

c. hats in the case _____   **f.** scarves _____

2. Put the words from the box in alphabetical order to complete the store directory.
Then look at the accessories. Write the correct display case number for each item.

purses   hats   necklaces   scarves   earrings   key chains
ties   handkerchiefs   belts   rings   wallets   pins   ~~backpacks~~
chains   watches   bracelets

STORE DIRECTORY

	Display case
backpacks	3
_____	6
_____	1
_____	2
_____	1
_____	9
_____	10
_____	7
_____	2
_____	4
_____	3
_____	4
_____	9
_____	5
_____	7
_____	8

__7__ a.

____ b.

____ c.

____ d.

____ e.

____ f.

____ g.

____ h.

____ i.

____ j.

____ k.

____ l.

____ m.

____ n.

____ o.

____ p.

68

3. Cross out the word that doesn't belong.

a. **Things you wear around your neck**   tie   ~~belt~~   scarf   locket

b. **Types of necklaces**   beads   bracelet   chain   pearls

c. **Things you can keep a change purse in**   backpack   shoulder bag   wallet   tote bag

d. **Types of shoes**   sandals   boots   pumps   suspenders

e. **Parts of a shoe**   sole   pin   heel   toe

4. Complete the ad. Use the words in the box.

track shoes	~~boots~~	high heels	hiking boots
loafers	oxfords	sandals	running shoes

The Good Sole SALE
Save 20% on men's and women's shoes

a. _boots_   b. _____   c. _____   d. _____

e. _____   f. _____   g. _____   h. _____

Located at the Lincoln Mall. Route 65.

5. What about you? Check (✓) the items you have.

☐ chain   ☐ watch   ☐ pierced earrings

☐ clip-on earrings   ☐ belt buckle   ☐ key chain

Challenge List the kinds of shoes you have. When do you wear them? **Example:** *boots—I wear them in cold or wet weather.*

Describing Clothes

1. Look at the yellow sweaters in your dictionary. **True** or **False**?

   a. They are new. _____True_____   **d.** They are long-sleeved. _____

   b. They have a V-neck. _____   **e.** They have stains. _____

   c. They come in four sizes. _____   **f.** They are checked. _____

2. Match the opposites. Write the number.

   _4_ **a.** new   **1.** plain

   ___ **b.** short   **2.** wide

   ___ **c.** formal   **3.** tight

   ___ **d.** fancy   **4.** old

   ___ **e.** heavy   **5.** low

   ___ **f.** loose   **6.** casual

   ___ **g.** narrow   **7.** light

   ___ **h.** high   **8.** long

3. Look at the pictures. Describe the problems. Use words from Exercise 2 and the word *too*.

  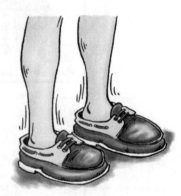

   a. They're _too short_.   **b.** They're _____.   **c.** They're _____.

   d. It's _____.   **e.** It's _____.

4. Look at the order form. Circle the correct words to complete the statements.

Item #	Page #	Description	Size	Colour	Quantity	Item Price	Total
563218	3	wool sweater	S	red and black striped	1	$15.00	$15.00
0421578	7	silk T-shirt	XS	light blue	1	17.00	17.00
962143	12	linen jacket	M	black	1	62.00	62.00
583614	8	rayon shirt	L	paisley	1	18.00	18.00
216983	10	loose-fit jeans	7	black	2	25.00	50.00

CLOTHES TOWN CATALOGUE STORE   ORDER TOLL-FREE 1-800-555-4627

a. The customer wants a <u>medium</u> /(small) sweater.

b. The customer wants a <u>long / large</u> paisley shirt.

c. The paisley shirt is <u>cotton / synthetic</u>.

d. The T-shirt is <u>solid / polka-dotted</u>.

e. The material of the jacket is <u>heavy / light</u>.

f. The jeans are <u>baggy / tight</u>.

5. What about you? Look at the ad. Choose two items to order. Add them to the order form in Exercise 4.

men's and women's
turtlenecks
S, M, L 100% cotton

men's and women's
V-neck sweaters
S, M, L 100% wool

308965 . . . .$18.00

843567 . . . . $32.00

page 39

Challenge   Describe the clothes you are wearing today. Include the colour and material.

Doing the Laundry

1. Look in your dictionary. Where is the…? Use *on* in your answer.

   a. bleach   <u> on the shelf </u>   **c.** spray starch   _____

   b. fabric softener   _____   **d.** pair of socks   _____

2. Match the pictures with the instructions. Write the number.

<u>5</u> **a.**

    1.   **Clean the lint trap!**

___ **b.**

    2.   **Iron the shirt!**

___ **c.**

    3.   **Fold the clothes!**

___ **d.**

    4.   **Unload the washer!**

___ **e.**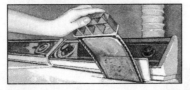

    5.   **Sort the clothes!**

___ **f.**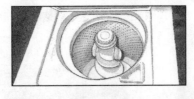

    6.   **Load the washer!**

___ **g.**

    7.   **Wash the shirt!**

Challenge   Think of five clothing items. How do you clean them? **Example:** *my jeans—I put them in the washer. Then I dry them on the clothesline.*

1. Look in your dictionary. Who said…?

a. **Please let out the waistband, too.**   _____customer_____

b. **I love this new sewing machine.**   _____

c. **I'm almost finished with this hemline.**   _____

2. Look at the pictures. Check (✓) the alterations the tailor made.

Altered States

- ☑ sew on buttons
- ☐ repair zipper
- ☐ lengthen hemline
- ☐ shorten hemline
- ☐ take in waistband
- ☐ let out waistband
- ☐ repair pocket
- ☐ repair seam

Before   **After**

3. List the items in the sewing basket. Include the number.

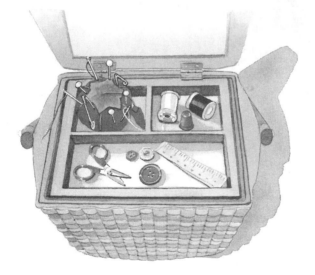

_____1 tape measure_____

_____

_____

_____

_____

_____

_____

_____

_____

Challenge Write about some clothing alterations. **Example:** *My jeans were too long. My cousin shortened them.*

▶ Go to page 174 for Another Look (Unit 5).

The Body

1. Look in your dictionary. Cross out the word that doesn't belong.

   a. **Face**   nose   jaw   chin   ~~neck~~

   b. **Inside the body** liver   intestines abdomen   stomach

   c. **The foot**   knee   heel   ankle   toe

   d. **The skeleton**   pelvis   rib cage   skull   brain

   e. **The hand**   finger   toenail   palm   wrist

   f. **The senses**   taste   see   ear   smell

2. Label the parts of the face. Use the words in the box.

ear	eye	eyebrow	eyelashes	eyelid	cheek	chin
forehead	gums	~~hair~~	jaw	lip	mouth	nose	teeth

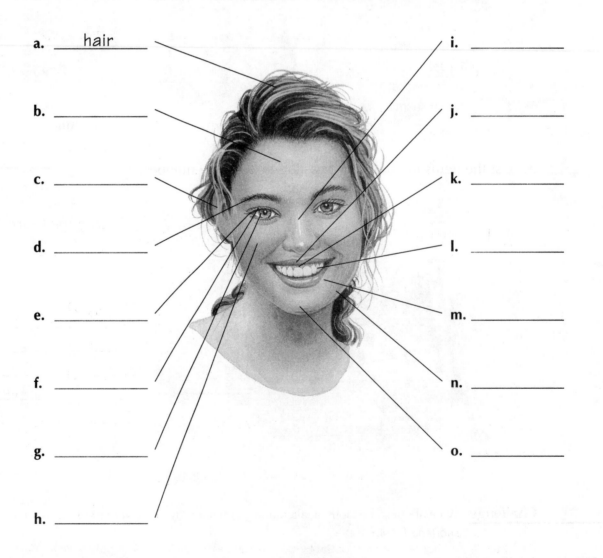

a. ___hair___

b. _____

c. _____

d. _____

e. _____

f. _____

g. _____

h. _____

i. _____

j. _____

k. _____

l. _____

m. _____

n. _____

o. _____

3. Look at the picture. Check (✓) the parts of the body that are NOT covered by clothes.

- ✓ arm
- ☐ back
- ☐ calves
- ☐ chest
- ☐ elbows
- ☐ fingers
- ☐ feet
- ☐ hands
- ☐ head
- ☐ knees
- ☐ legs
- ☐ neck
- ☐ shoulders
- ☐ waist

4. Look at the picture. Match the words with the parts of the body. Write the number.

<u>4</u> **a.** heart
___ **b.** kidney
___ **c.** lung
___ **d.** liver
___ **e.** gallbladder
___ **f.** bladder
___ **g.** throat
___ **h.** stomach
___ **i.** pancreas
___ **j.** brain
___ **k.** intestines

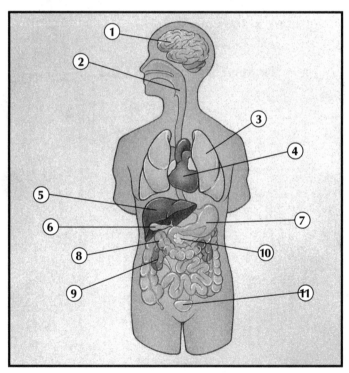

5. What about you? <u>Underline</u> the parts of the body that are NOT OK for men to show on the street in your country. Circle the parts of the body that are NOT OK for women.

| arms | abdomen | elbows | face | hair | mouth |
| shoulders | back | chest | knees | calves | feet |

Challenge Choose five parts of the body. What are their functions? **Example:** *brain—We use it to think.*

Personal Hygiene

1. Look in your dictionary. Cross out the word that doesn't belong.

a.	shower cap	soap	~~hair spray~~	talcum powder
b.	electric shaver	razor blade	aftershave	sunscreen
c.	hair clip	emery board	polish	polish remover
d.	barrettes	eyebrow pencil	clips	hair gel
e.	blush	foundation	eyeliner	deodorant
f.	moisturizer	shampoo	blow dryer	conditioner
g.	toothbrush	comb	dental floss	toothpaste

2. Look at Exercise 1. Write the letter of the items that you need for these activities.

_d_ **1.** do your hair   ___ **5.** shave

___ **2.** take a shower   ___ **6.** wash your hair

___ **3.** put on makeup   ___ **7.** brush your teeth

___ **4.** do your nails

3. Look at the checklist. Check (✓) the items that Teresa packed.

Travel Packing List

✓ blow dryer	☐ mascara
☐ bobby pins	☐ mouthwash
☐ brush	☐ nail clipper
☐ cologne/perfume	☐ nail polish
☐ comb	☐ shampoo
☐ conditioner	☐ shaving cream
☐ curling iron	☐ shower cap
☐ dental floss	☐ soap
☐ deodorant	☐ sunscreen
☐ electric shaver/razor	☐ talcum powder
☐ emery board	☐ toothbrush
☐ lipstick	☐ toothpaste

4. Teresa is at a hotel. Look at the items the hotel gives guests. Go back to the checklist in Exercise 3. Check (✓) the additional items that Teresa now has.

5. What does Teresa still need? Complete her shopping list.

HOTEL KENT

To Buy

bobby pins
_____
_____
_____
_____
_____
_____
_____

6. What about you? Which items do you use? Check (✓) the correct column.

	EVERY DAY	SOMETIMES	NEVER
sunscreen			
cologne			
conditioner			
hair spray			
dental floss			
body lotion			
moisturizer			
Other: _____			

Challenge List the personal hygiene items you take with you when you travel.

1. Look in your dictionary. **True** or **False**?

   a. The woman in bed has chills.   _____True_____

   b. The man in 11 has an insect bite on his right arm.   _____

   c. The man in 13 has a cut on his thumb.   _____

   d. The man in 14 didn't use enough sunscreen.   _____

   e. The man in 15 has a blister on his left hand.   _____

   f. The young man with a handkerchief has a bloody nose.   _____

   g. The woman in 18 sprained her right ankle.   _____

2. Look at Tania's medicine. Complete the form. (You can look at **page 81** in your dictionary for help.)

   Patient's name: _____Tania Zobor_____

   Please check (✓) all the symptoms you have.

   I often get...
   ☐ headaches   ☐ earaches   ☑ toothaches   ☐ stomachaches   ☐ backaches
   ☐ sore throats   ☐ nasal congestion   ☐ fevers   ☐ bruises   ☐ rashes

   I often...
   ☐ cough   ☐ sneeze   ☐ feel naseous   ☐ feel dizzy   ☐ vomit

3. What about you? Complete the form for yourself or someone you know.

   Patient's name: _____

   Please check (✓) all the symptoms you have.

   I often get...
   ☐ headaches   ☐ earaches   ☐ toothaches   ☐ stomachaches   ☐ backaches
   ☐ sore throats   ☐ nasal congestion   ☐ fevers   ☐ bruises   ☐ rashes

   I often...
   ☐ cough   ☐ sneeze   ☐ feel naseous   ☐ feel dizzy   ☐ vomit

Challenge What can you do for the health problems in Exercise 3? **Example:** *headaches—take pain reliever*

1. Look at the bottom picture in your dictionary. Write the name of the part of the body.

   a. asthma   <u>lungs</u>   **d.** TB   <u>   </u>

   b. high blood pressure <u>   </u>   **e.** intestinal parasites <u>   </u>

   c. diabetes   <u>   </u>   **f.** HIV   <u>   </u>

2. Look at the photos of Mehmet when he was a child. Complete the form.

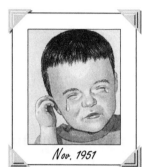

Nov. 1951   *Jan. 1953*   *Dec. 1959*   *May 1964*

Name <u>Mehmet Caner</u>   Date of birth <u>April 18, 1949</u>

Check (✓) the illnesses or conditions you had as a child.

☐ measles   ☐ chicken pox   ☐ mumps

☐ asthma   ☐ allergies   ☑ ear infections

3. What about you? Complete the form for yourself or someone you know.

Name <u>   </u>   Date of birth <u>   </u>

Check (✓) the illnesses or conditions you had as a child.

☐ measles   ☐ chicken pox   ☐ mumps

☐ asthma   ☐ allergies   ☐ ear infections

Challenge List the things you do when you have a cold or the flu. **Example:** *drink hot water with lemon*

1. Look in your dictionary. Who said...?

a. ⟨ **Your prescription is ready.** ⟩   _pharmacist_

b. ⟨ **The brace is helping you walk better.** ⟩   _____

c. ⟨ **These glasses will look nice on you.** ⟩   _____

d. ⟨ **This hearing aid will help.** ⟩   _____

e. ⟨ **This cast stays on for six weeks.** ⟩   _____

2. Look at Dr. Burns's notes for Brian, a patient injured in an accident. **True** or **False**?

> From the desk of
> **Dr. Mary Burns**
>
> 1. Use heating pad on arm.
> 2. Take over-the-counter pain reliever when needed.
> 3. Exercise every day.
> 4. Fill prescription for tetracycline.
> 5. Use cane for 4 weeks.
> 6. Call for appointment in 2 weeks.

a. This is a prescription.   _False_

b. Brian must get bed rest.   _____

c. He can't exercise.   _____

d. He can use a heating pad.   _____

e. He needs a humidifier.   _____

f. He must take medicine.   _____

g. He needs crutches.   _____

3. What do you need for each problem? Write the number in the blank.

   _4_ a. legally blind   **1.** wheelchair

   _____ b. broken arm   **2.** crutches

   _____ c. paralysis   **3.** heating pad

   _____ d. broken leg   **4.** white cane

   _____ e. back pain   **5.** sling

4. Look at the picture. Circle the words to complete the statements.

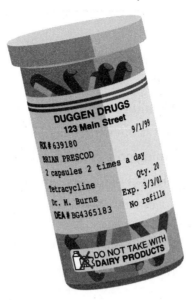

DUGGEN DRUGS
123 Main Street   9/1/99

RX# 639180
BRIAN PRESCOD
2 capsules 2 times a day   Qty. 20
Tetracycline   Exp. 3/3/01
Dr. M. Burns
DEA# BG4365183   No refills

DO NOT TAKE WITH DAIRY PRODUCTS

a. Brian went to the chiropractor / ⟨pharmacy.⟩

b. He got over-the-counter medication / prescription medication.

c. The bottle contains capsules / tablets.

d. The prescription label / warning label reads "Do not take with dairy products."

e. Brian can't drink fluids / eat cheese with this medicine.

f. The dosage / expiry date is two pills twice a day.

g. The medicine isn't good after September 1999 / March 2001.

5. What about you? Check (✔) the items you <u>think</u> are in your medicine cabinet. Then check your answers at home.

☐ pain reliever

☐ cold tablets

☐ antacid

☐ vitamins

☐ cough syrup

☐ throat lozenges

☐ nasal spray

☐ ointment

☐ eye drops

☐ Other: _____

Challenge Look at some prescription or over-the-counter medication in your medicine cabinet. What's the dosage? The expiry date? Is there a warning label? Make a list.

Medical Emergencies

1. Look in your dictionary. **True** or **False**?

a. The girl under the blue blanket is injured.   ___True___

b. The man in the yellow shirt is hurt, too.   _____

c. The man in the red shirt is having an allergic reaction.   _____

d. The child in the swimming pool is unconscious.   _____

e. The woman at the table is choking on a fish bone.   _____

f. The boy in the doctor's office broke a leg.   _____

2. Look at the chart. How did the people injure themselves? Circle the best answer.

NUMBER OF CLAIMS FOR INJURIES		Maybe people….
sprains or strains	46 439	(fell) / choked **a.**
cuts or lacerations	9 109	bled / overdosed **b.**
fractures	7 203	drowned / broke bones **c.**
burns	1 720	got blisters / had allergies **d.**
poisonings	397	coughed / swallowed poison **e.**
contact with electrical current	151	got a shock / couldn't breathe **f.**
freezing	10	were burned / got frostbite **g.**

Workplace Safety and Insurance Board of Ontario
1997 Statistics (Tables 6 and 8)

3. What about you? Check (✓) the emergencies that have happened to you. When or where did they happen?

EMERGENCY	WHEN?/WHERE?
☐ I had an allergic reaction to _____ .	_____
☐ I got frostbite.	_____
☐ I fell.	_____
☐ I broke my _____ .	_____
☐ Other: _____ .	_____

Challenge   Write a paragraph about an emergency in Exercise 3. What treatment did you get?
Look at **page 83** in your dictionary for help.

1. Look in your dictionary. Write the first aid item for these conditions.

    a. broken finger   _____splint_____

    b. rash on hand   _____

    c. swollen foot   _____ or _____

    d. infected cut   _____ or _____

2. Look at the items from Chen's first aid kit. Check (✓) the items he has.

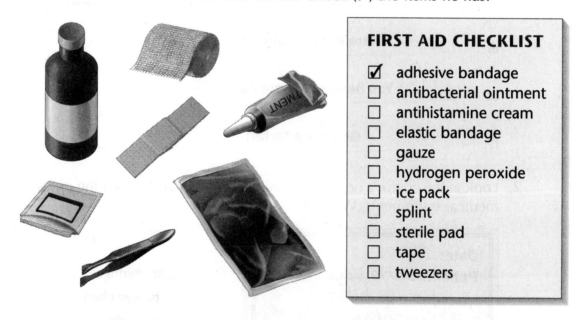

FIRST AID CHECKLIST

- ☑ adhesive bandage
- ☐ antibacterial ointment
- ☐ antihistamine cream
- ☐ elastic bandage
- ☐ gauze
- ☐ hydrogen peroxide
- ☐ ice pack
- ☐ splint
- ☐ sterile pad
- ☐ tape
- ☐ tweezers

3. What about you? Check (✓) the first aid items you <u>think</u> you have at home. Then check your answers at home.

FIRST AID CHECKLIST

- ☐ adhesive bandage
- ☐ antibacterial ointment
- ☐ antihistamine cream
- ☐ elastic bandage
- ☐ gauze
- ☐ hydrogen peroxide
- ☐ ice pack
- ☐ splint
- ☐ sterile pad
- ☐ tape
- ☐ tweezers

DO YOU KNOW HOW TO DO...?	YES	NO
the Heimlich manoeuvre		
CPR		
artificial respiration		

Challenge Look at the items in Exercise 3. What can you use them for? **Example:**
adhesive bandages—cuts

Clinics

1. Look in your dictionary. Who said…?

   a. **Your pressure is very good.** ___nurse___

   b. **I'll give you a medical information form, Mr. Sun.** _____

   c. **In a month, no more braces, Ryan!** _____

   d. **Here's my health card.** _____

   e. **You have one more cavity.** _____

   f. **Good-bye tartar!** _____

2. Look at the doctor's notes. What did the doctor use? Match the notes with the medical instruments. Write the number.

   Date: 3/5/02
   Patient: Carla Vega
   1. weight—61 kilos
   2. B.P.—120/80
   3. temp.—37°
   4. lungs—clear
   5. vision—20/20
      (doesn't need glasses)
   6. gave flu vaccination

   ___ **a.** syringe
   ___ **b.** eye chart
   _1_ **c.** scale
   ___ **d.** thermometer
   ___ **e.** blood pressure gauge
   ___ **f.** stethoscope

3. What about you? Think of the last time you saw the doctor. How long were you…?

   in the waiting room   _____

   in the examining room   _____

   on the examination table   _____

Challenge Find out about health insurance in other countries. Which countries have national health insurance? Who can get it?

1. Look in your dictionary. **True** or **False**?

   a. Picture A: The man is making an appointment to see the doctor.   <u>True</u>

   b. Picture B: The nurse is checking the patient's blood pressure.   _____

   c. Picture C: The doctor is examining the patient's mouth.   _____

   d. Picture F: The doctor is looking in the patient's ears.   _____

   e. Picture K: The dentist is drilling a tooth.   _____

2. Write the words under the correct pictures.

clean teeth	draw blood	examine eyes	fill a cavity
give a shot	pull a tooth	take an X-ray	take ~~temperature~~

  a. <u>take temperature</u>   **b.** _____   **c.** _____

 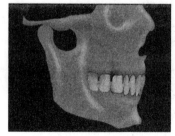 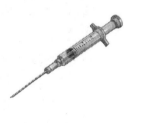

  d. _____   **e.** _____   **f.** _____

 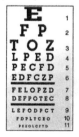

  g. _____   **h.** _____

Challenge Look at **page 184** in this book. Complete the diagram.

A Hospital

1. Look at the patient's room in your dictionary. What should a patient use who…?
   a. wants to eat breakfast _____ *bed table* _____
   b. wants to sit up in the hospital bed _____
   c. doesn't have pyjamas _____
   d. can't walk to the bathroom _____
   e. wants a nurse _____

2. Look at the two lists. Match the patients with the hospital staff. Write the number.

PATIENTS			4/7/01
Name	**Age**	**Room**	**Condition**
2 a. Ellen Lee	25	243	pregnant
___ b. Tom Lyons	17	265	nervous, confused
___ c. Chris Baker	6	284	chicken pox
___ d. Allen Rogers	80	364	eye pain
___ e. Marta Varga	53	398	diabetes *requested clean sheets*
___ f. Tony Petchak	49	298	HIV *blood test scheduled*
___ g. Arthur Lewin	75	376	heart attack
___ h. Ilsa Grueber	63	378	intestinal parasites
___ i. Annie Minkoff	78	249	broken hip *X-rays scheduled*

HOSPITAL STAFF	4/7/01
1. Dr. James Cranston	internist
2. Dr. Mary Ferguson	obstetrician
3. Dr. Robert Hecht	ophthalmologist
4. Dr. Carmen Rivera	pediatrician
5. Dr. Doug London	psychiatrist
6. Dr. Mei-hua Chang	cardiologist
7. Charlie Olsen	X-ray technician
8. Joan Osborne	lab technician
9. Billy Parker	orderly

3. Look in your dictionary. Who's...?

a. standing near the vital signs monitor   _____nurse_____

b. taking flowers to a patient   _____

c. carrying a medication tray   _____

d. talking to the dietician   _____

e. pushing a gurney   _____

f. lying on the operating table   _____

g. wearing glasses   _____

h. helping the surgeon   _____

i. in the operating room with the surgeon and the nurse   _____

4. Match the objects in the supply room with the items on the supplies list. Write the number.

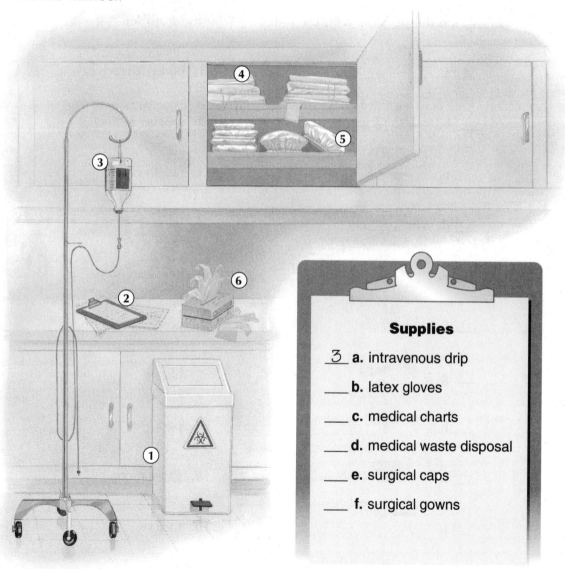

Supplies

_3_ **a.** intravenous drip

___ **b.** latex gloves

___ **c.** medical charts

___ **d.** medical waste disposal

___ **e.** surgical caps

___ **f.** surgical gowns

Challenge   Find out the names of an internist, an ophthalmologist, and a pediatrician in your community. Make a list.

▶ **Go to page 175 for Another Look (Unit 6).**

City Streets

1. Look in your dictionary. Circle the correct words to complete the sentences.

   a. There's a (furniture store) / hardware store on Main and Elm.

   b. There's <u>a movie theatre / an office building</u> on First and Elm.

   c. The <u>mosque / synagogue</u> is on Second and Oak.

   d. The <u>car dealership / parking garage</u> is next to the high-rise building.

   e. The <u>fire station / police station</u> is on Main and Oak.

   f. There's a <u>hotel / motel</u> on Pine and Second.

   g. The <u>city hall / courthouse</u> is on Main and Pine.

   h. There's a woman in front of the <u>bakery / bank</u>.

2. Match the pictures with the places. Write the number.

<u>2</u> a.   1. barber shop

___ b.    2. grocery store

___ c.   3. health club

___ d. ⬛━━⬛   4. bank

___ e.   5. hardware store

___ f.   6. post office

___ g.   7. library

___ h.   8. park

___ i.   9. gas station

___ j.   10. theatre

___ k.   11. coffee shop

___ l.   12. fire station

3. Look at the map. Complete the notes.

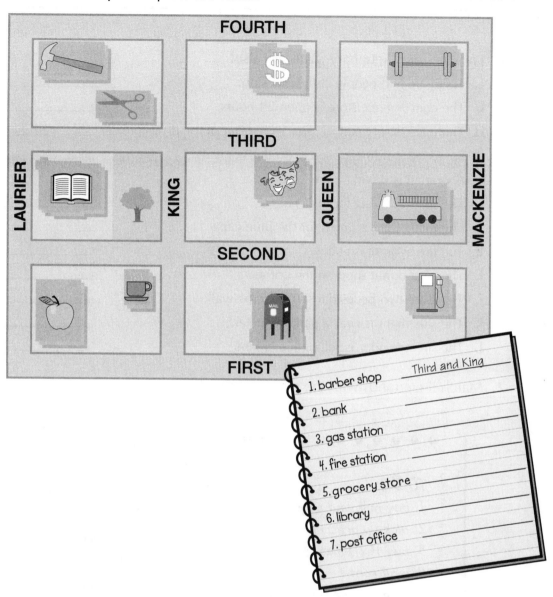

FOURTH

THIRD

SECOND

FIRST

LAURIER   KING   QUEEN   MACKENZIE

1. barber shop   _Third and King_
2. bank _____
3. gas station _____
4. fire station _____
5. grocery store _____
6. library _____
7. post office _____

4. What about you? Write the street locations for these places in your community.

school   _____

library   _____

post office   _____

hospital   _____

fire station   _____

police station   _____

Other: _____

Challenge   Draw a street map of an area you know. Include the location of some places from Exercise 2.

An Intersection

1. Look in your dictionary. **True** or **False**?

   a. There are two people at the bus stop.   <u>   True   </u>

   b. The convenience store is open 24 hours.   _____

   c. There are empty parking spaces in front of the drugstore.   _____

   d. Someone is riding a bicycle on the sidewalk.   _____

   e. A woman is driving a grey car.   _____

   f. The bus is waiting for the light.   _____

   g. The traffic light is green for the blue car.   _____

   h. The fire hydrant is yellow.   _____

   i. There's a donut shop on the corner.   _____

   j. There are two pedestrians in the crosswalk.   _____

   k. The streetlight is near a parking meter.   _____

   l. The street vendor is selling ice cream.   _____

2. Match the errands with the places. Write the number.

   TO DO:

   1. buy milk and eggs
   2. pick up prescription
   3. buy the Times
   4. mail rent
   5. meet Meng for lunch
   6. pick up raincoat
   7. drop off roll of film
   8. copy English paper
   9. wash sheets and towels
   10. call Olga at 5:30

   ___ a. photo shop

   ___ b. public telephone

   ___ c. dry cleaners

   ___ d. copy centre

   ___ e. drugstore

   ___ f. Laundromat

   <u>1</u> g. convenience store

   ___ h. fast food restaurant

   ___ i. newsstand

   ___ j. mailbox

3. Cross out the word that doesn't belong.

a. People	pedestrian	street vendor	~~corner~~
b. Stores	donut shop	mailbox	pharmacy
c. Services	bicycle	Laundromat	nail salon
d. Transportation	parking space	bus	motorcycle
e. Parts of the street	curb	crosswalk	drive-thru window
f. Things you put coins in	public telephone	parking meter	fire hydrant
g. Things that move	sign	cart	garbage truck

4. Write the location of these signs. Use words from Exercise 3.

a. _____Laundromat_____

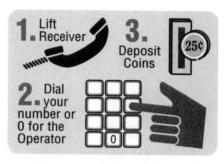

b. _____

c. _____

d. _____

French Fries $1.00
   with cheese $1.50
Hamburger $3.00
Cheeseburger $3.50
   Lettuce & Tomato .... 50¢
Popcorn $1.35
Gum .... 65¢

e. _____

First Mail pick-up	8:30 AM
Next pick-up	10:30 AM
Next pick-up	1:30 PM
Next pick-up	4:30 PM
Final Mail pick-up	7:30 PM

f. _____

5. What about you? Make a list of neighbourhood errands and locations. Use your own paper.

Example: *pick up prescription—drugstore*

Challenge Look in your dictionary. Write the locations of five stores. **Example:** *The donut shop is on the corner.*

91

A Mall

1. Look in your dictionary. Where can you buy these items? Do not use *department store*.

a. ___card store___

b. _____

c. _____

d. _____

e. _____

f. _____

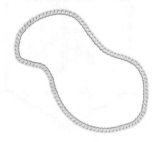

g. _____

h. _____

i. _____

2. Look in your dictionary. Complete the mall directory.

MALL DIRECTORY			
Cards/Books	**Floor**	**Services**	**Floor**
card store	1	optician	___
_____	___	_____	___
		_____	___
Department Store	1, 2		
Entertainment/Music		**Shoes/Accessories**	
_____	___	_____	___
_____	___	_____	___
Food		**Specialty Stores**	
_____	___	pet store	___
_____	___	_____	___
_____	___	_____	___

3. Look at this mall directory and map. Circle the words to complete the conversations.

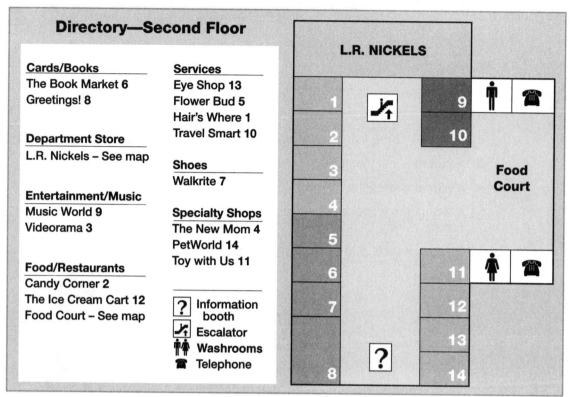

Customer 1: Excuse me. Where's the bookstore?

Information: It's next to the pet store / (shoe store.)
                                 a.

Customer 2: Can you tell me where the hair salon is?

Information: Sure. It's next to the department store / information booth.
                                                  b.

Customer 3: I'm looking for the escalator / women's washroom.
                                           c.

Information: It's in front of Nickel's.

Customer 4: Hi. Where's the travel agency, please?

Information: It's right over there. Next to the toy store / music store.
                                                  d.

Customer 5: Excuse me. I'm looking for the candy store.

Information: It's between the music store / video store and the hair salon / maternity shop.
                                         e.   **f.**

Customer 6: Excuse me. Is there an optician in this mall?

Information: Yes. There's one across from the card store / candy store.
                                               g.

Challenge Look at the map in Exercise 3. Write the locations of Videorama, the men's washroom, Flower Bud, and PetWorld.

93

A Childcare Centre

1. Look at the top picture in your dictionary. **True** or **False**?

   a. A childcare worker is dropping off a little girl. ___False___

   b. A girl is playing with toys. _____

   c. The girl in blue jeans is taking a nap. _____

   d. A parent is changing diapers. _____

   e. A parent is dressing his son. _____

   f. A woman in a rocking chair is reading a story. _____

2. Match the words that go together. Write the number.

   _4_ a. high   1. ring

   ___ b. diaper   2. table

   ___ c. teething   3. pin

   ___ d. cloth   4. chair

   ___ e. change   5. diaper

3. What is it? Complete the sentences. Use the words from Exercise 2.

   a. A baby sits in it. ___a high chair___

   b. A baby puts it in its mouth. _____

   c. A disposable diaper doesn't need it. _____

   d. A baby lies on it. _____

   e. A baby wears it. _____

4. What about you? Have you ever...? Check (✔) the correct column.

	YES	NO
held a baby		
read a story to a child		
fed a child		
dressed a child		
changed a diaper		
rocked a baby to sleep		

5. Cross out the word that doesn't belong. You can use your dictionary for help.

a. **People**	parent	childcare worker	~~pacifier~~
b. **Places to sit**	high chair	diaper pail	potty seat
c. **Things a baby wears**	walker	bib	diaper
d. **Things to feed a baby**	formula	baby food	disinfectant
e. **Things that have wheels**	rocking chair	carriage	stroller
f. **Things to put in a baby's mouth**	teething ring	cubby	nipple
g. **Things for changing diapers**	baby powder	playpen	wipes
h. **Things a baby plays with**	baby backpack	rattles	toys
i. **Things that hold a baby**	diaper pins	baby carrier	car safety seat

6. There are 12 childcare words. They go → and ↓. Find and circle them.

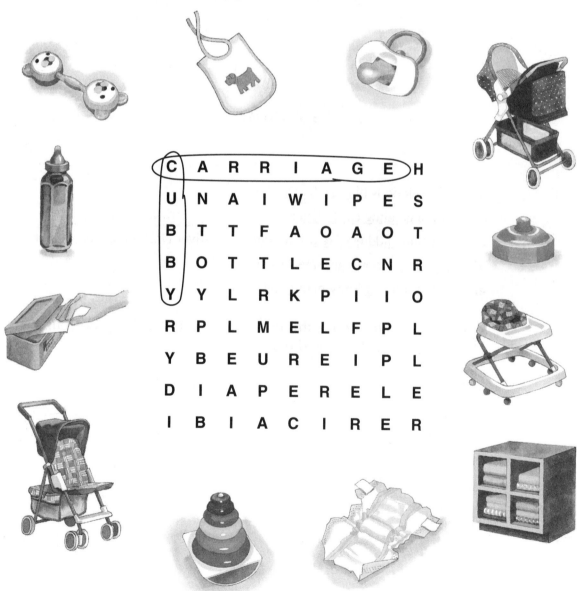

Challenge Rewrite the false sentences in Exercise 1. Make them true.

Canada Post

1. Look in your dictionary. **True** or **False**?

   a. The letter carrier delivers mail.   ___True___

   b. The postcard has a return address.   _____

   c. You can send a package by parcel post.   _____

   d. The airmail envelope is white.   _____

   e. You can receive Express Post the next day.   _____

2. Circle the correct words to complete the sentences.

   a. The envelope is blue / (white.)

   b. This is a greeting card / letter.

   c. The mailing address / return address is 65 River Dr., Birchwood, Manitoba, D4E 5F6.

   d. The postage / postmark says December 15.

   e. Alicia sent this priority mail / registered mail.

3. What about you? Address this envelope to your teacher. Use your school's address. Don't forget your return address.

Challenge Find out how much it costs to send a letter, a postcard, and an airmail letter.

96

1. Look in your dictionary. Circle the words to complete the sentences.

   a. The security guard / (teller) is speaking to a man.

   b. The man has cash / a passbook in his hand.

   c. The bank machine / vault is behind the teller.

   d. The cheque book / safety-deposit box is light green.

   e. The deposit slip is about the same size as the bank card / cheque book.

2. Look at the bank receipt. **True** or **False**?

   a. This is a monthly statement.   _____False_____

   b. The customer used a bank
      machine (ATM).   _____

   c. She made a deposit.   _____

   d. She withdrew $100 from her
      chequing account.   _____

   e. Her savings account number
      is 056588734.   _____

   f. Her balance is $623.40.   _____

   FIRST BANK
   54 CHURCH STREET
   KINGSTON, ON

   DATE: 05/06/99   TIME: 11:51
   ATM : 045-3
   CARD NUMBER: ************6434

   TRANSACTION: WITHDRAWAL
   SERIAL NUM.:   345
   AMOUNT: $100.00
   FROM SAVINGS: 056588734
   BALANCE: $6234

3. Imagine you want to transfer forty dollars from your savings account to your chequing account. Look at the ATM screens. Circle the correct transaction for each screen.

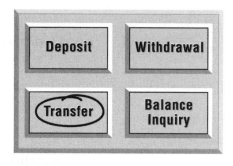

a.

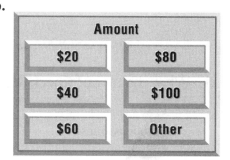

b.

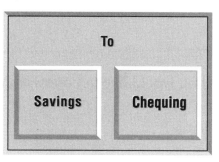

c.   d.

Challenge   Rewrite the false sentences in Exercise 2. Make them true.

A Library

1. Look in your dictionary. Where can you find...?

a. titles and locations of library books   in the   <u>online catalogue</u>

                                                or   _____

b. magazines and newspapers   in the   _____

c. maps   in an   _____

d. records and CDs   in the   _____

e. the library clerk   at the   _____

f. the reference librarian   at the   _____

2. Look at the chart. Complete the sentences.

Public Library—Holdings

a. There are 724 <u>compact discs</u> in the library.

b. The library has 43 different kinds of _____ and 6 different kinds of

   _____ .

c. There are 3 _____ .

d. The library has almost 70 000 _____ .

e. There are 2 sets of _____ .

f. The library has almost 2000 _____ and a little more than 2000

   _____ .

g. There are almost 900 _____ .

3. What about you? Check (✓) the items you would like to borrow from a library.

☐ books   ☐ records   ☐ CDs

☐ audiocassettes   ☐ videocassettes   ☐ Other: _____

Challenge   Go to your school library or a local library. Where are the items you checked in Exercise 3? For how long can you borrow them?

1. Look in your dictionary. Circle the words to complete the sentences.

    a. The <u>guard</u> / <u>police officer</u> arrested the suspect.

    b. The <u>suspect / witness</u> wears handcuffs.

    c. The <u>defence lawyer / Crown counsel</u> is a man.

    d. The <u>court reporter / judge</u> says "guilty."

    e. There are <u>ten / twelve</u> people on the jury.

    f. The <u>convict / bailiff</u> is in prison.

2. Complete the sentences with the words in the box. Then number the events in order.

court	defendant	~~jail~~	lawyer	released
	suspect	trial	verdict	

    ___ **a.** The defendant goes to _____jail_____.

    ___ **b.** The defendant stands _____.

    ___ **c.** The judge sentences the _____.

    ___ **d.** The defendant appears in _____.

    ___ **e.** The convict is _____.

    ___ **f.** The judge gives the _____.

    _1_ **g.** The police officer arrests a _____.

    ___ **h.** The suspect hires a _____.

3. Label the items. Use the words in the box.

bail	evidence	~~handcuffs~~

a. _____handcuffs_____   **b.** _____   **c.** _____

Challenge Look in your dictionary. Tell the story. **Begin:** *The police officer arrested the suspect…*

Crime

1. Look in your dictionary. Read the TV movie descriptions. Circle all the crime words.

② **Under the Influence ('89)** Forrest March, Jill Gilmore. (Drunk driving) destroys two families.

④ **The Necklace ('95)** Rob Philip, Seth Jackson. A burglary changes life in a small, quiet town.

⑤ **Crimes Against Property ('99)** Anna Lauck, Sam Hull, Evan Scott. A family is shocked when their teenage son is arrested for vandalism.

⑦ **The Victim ('88)** Elisa Rivera, Bill Delany. Woman fights back during a mugging.

⑨ **The Candy Shop ('93)** Tom Ryder, Amara Dee. Police find teenagers selling illegal drugs.

⑬ **Keep the Change ('97)** Liza Moore, Dean Adams. A brutal assault changes a man's life.

㉘ **East Side Saga ('93)** Brian Terry, Johnny Ray Lone. A story of gang violence.

㊶ **The Last Breakfast ('90)** Lon Matheson, Verna Tiler. A doctor is arrested for her husband's murder.

2. Match the TV movies with the descriptions in Exercise 1. Write the channel number.

a. 28

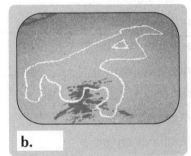

b.

c.

d.

e.

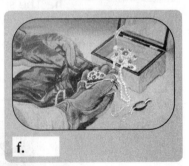

f.

g.

h.

Challenge Look at the TV listings in a newspaper or TV program guide. Which programs are about crimes? Which types of crimes?

1. Look in your dictionary. **True** or **False**?

a. The girls on the street are friends. _____True_____

b. The women on the subway are holding their purses close to their bodies. _____

c. The elderly woman is opening the door to a stranger. _____

d. The taxi driver is drinking and driving. _____

e. The elderly man is reporting a crime. _____

2. Match the problems with the advice. Write the number.

_5_ **a.**

1. Hold your purse close to your body!

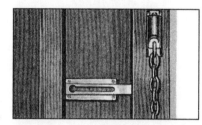

___ **b.**

2. Walk with a friend!

___ **c.**

3. Protect your wallet!

___ **d.**

4. Lock your door!

___ **e.**

5. Stay on well-lit streets!

Challenge Make a list of steps you take to be safe in public.

Emergencies and Natural Disasters

1. Look in your dictionary. Write the disaster or emergency.

a. It's covering the house!   _mudslide_

b. It's going to hit the farm!   _____

c. We need rain.   _____

d. Don't move. We're coming to get you!   _____

e. The light was red! You didn't stop!   _____

f. Mindy! Mindy! Where are you, Mindy?   _____

g. There's almost a metre of snow!   _____

Key:
airplane crash   flood
forest fire   blizzard
hurricane   tornado

2. Look at the map. Answer the questions.

a. What happened near Peggy's Cove?   _airplane crash_

b. Where was there a blizzard?   _____

c. What happened near Nakina?   _____

d. What happened in Winnipeg?   _____

e. Where did a tornado occur?   _____

f. What big city felt the effect of a hurricane?   _____

3. Match the photos with the newspaper headlines. Write the number.

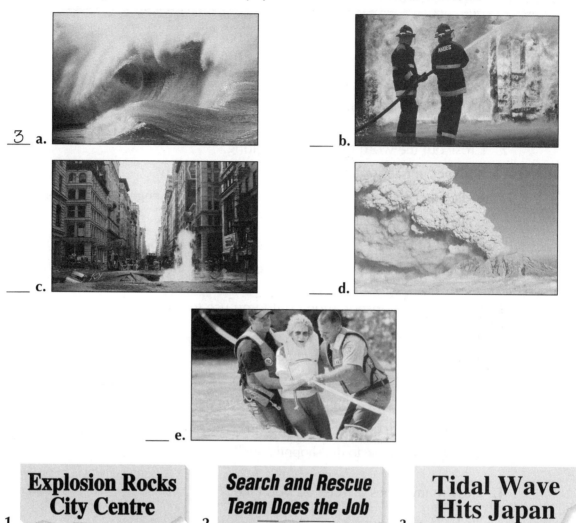

_3_ **a.**

___ **b.**

___ **c.**

___ **d.**

___ **e.**

1. **Explosion Rocks City Centre**

2. **Search and Rescue Team Does the Job**

3. **Tidal Wave Hits Japan**

4. **Fire Fighters Fight Flames**

5. *Volcanic Eruption At Mt. St. Helens*

4. What about you? Which natural disasters have you experienced? Complete the chart.

	WHERE?	WHEN?
earthquake		
blizzard		
hurricane		
tornado		
flood		
Other: _____		

Challenge Find information about a natural disaster. Look in an almanac, an encyclopedia, or a newspaper. What kind of disaster was it? Where and when did it happen?

▶ **Go to page 176 for Another Look (Unit 7).**

1. Look in your dictionary. How many … can you see?

   a. people at the bus stop   _2_   **c.** taxis at the taxi stand   _____

   b. passengers on the bus   _____   **d.** buses on the ferry   _____

2. Cross out the word that doesn't belong.

a. Types of transportation	bus	ferry	subway	~~ticket~~
b. People	bus driver	passenger	transfer	conductor
c. Forms of payment	fare	track	token	transit pass
d. Places to wait	passenger	platform	bus stop	train station
e. Things to read	schedule	train	route	meter

3. What public transportation could you use to travel…?

   a. from Edmonton to Halifax   _____

   b. from your house to your school   _____

   c. from Toronto to Montréal   _____

   d. from your house to the convenience store   _____

   e. from Nova Scotia to Newfoundland   _____

   f. from your house to the shopping mall   _____

4. How many times a week do you take:

   a. a bus   _____

   b. a train   _____

   c. a taxi   _____

   d. a walk of more than one kilometre   _____

   e. a subway   _____

Challenge Look at **page 184** in this book. Follow the instructions.

1. Look in your dictionary. **True** or **False**?

    a. The ferry is going under the bridge.   _False_

    b. A woman is getting into the taxi.   _____

    c. A man is getting out of the front of the taxi.   _____

    d. A red car is getting onto the highway.   _____

    e. A green car is getting off the highway.   _____

    f. There are two people going down the stairs.   _____

    g. A taxi is going through the tunnel.   _____

2. Look at the map. Circle the correct words to complete the directions.

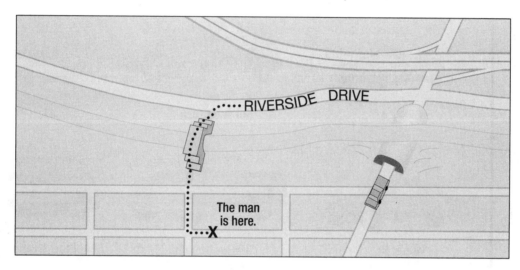

Man: Excuse me. How do I get to Riverside Drive?

Woman: Riverside Drive? Go around the (corner) / tunnel. Then go <u>down / up</u> the
                                                         a.   **b.**

        stairs and <u>over / under</u> the <u>bridge / highway</u>. Go <u>down / up</u> the stairs and you'll
                  c.   **d.**   **e.**

        be right on Riverside Drive.

Man: Oh, so I have to go <u>across / around</u> the bridge?
                                   f.

Woman: That's right.

3. Read the conversation in Exercise 2 again. Circle the correct answer.

    The man is <u>in a taxi / on a bus / walking</u>.

Challenge   Write directions to get from your home to school.

Cars and Trucks

1. Look in your dictionary. Circle the correct words to complete the sentences.

   a. The compact / subcompact is red.

   b. The RV / station wagon is beige.

   c. The dump truck / tow truck has a red stripe.

   d. The moving van / tractor trailer has an orange cab.

2. Look at the chart. Match the car models with the kinds of cars. Write the number.

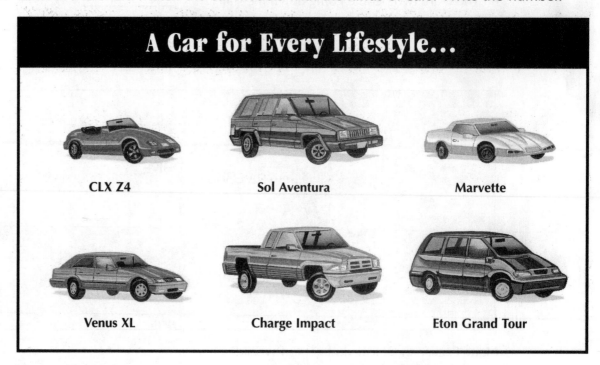

A Car for Every Lifestyle...

CLX Z4   Sol Aventura   Marvette

Venus XL   Charge Impact   Eton Grand Tour

   _5_ a. Venus XL   1. minivan

   ___ b. Marvette   2. sport utility vehicle

   ___ c. Charge Impact   3. pickup truck

   ___ d. Eton Grand Tour   4. sports car

   ___ e. Sol Aventura   5. midsize car

   ___ f. CLX Z4   6. convertible

3. What about you? Which car do you like? Choose one from Exercise 2.

   Colour: _____   Model: _____

Challenge Explain your choice in Exercise 3. **Example:** *I like the Eton Grand Tour minivan because I have a big family.*

1. Look at the intersection on **pages 90 and 91** in your dictionary. **True** or **False**?
   (*Note:* The Burger Queen is on the southwest corner.)

   a. Mel's Donuts is on the northeast corner.   _____True_____

   b. The convertible is going west.   _____

   c. The bicycle is going east.   _____

   d. The bus is going north.   _____

   e. The dry cleaners and the nail salon are on the same block. _____

   f. There's a stop sign at the intersection.   _____

   g. There's a "no parking" sign near the park.   _____

   h. There's a pedestrian crossing sign at the northwest corner. _____

   i. The motorcycle is on a one-way street.   _____

   j. There's handicapped parking in front of the dry cleaners. _____

   k. There aren't any speed limit signs.   _____

2. Look at the map. Use your pen or pencil to follow the directions to a shoe store. Put an X on the shoe store.

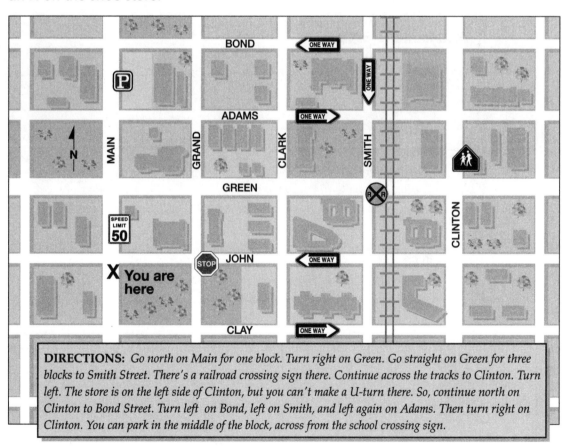

DIRECTIONS: *Go north on Main for one block. Turn right on Green. Go straight on Green for three blocks to Smith Street. There's a railroad crossing sign there. Continue across the tracks to Clinton. Turn left. The store is on the left side of Clinton, but you can't make a U-turn there. So, continue north on Clinton to Bond Street. Turn left on Bond, left on Smith, and left again on Adams. Then turn right on Clinton. You can park in the middle of the block, across from the school crossing sign.*

_____ **Challenge** Give directions to a place near your school. Draw a map.

Parts of a Car and Car Maintenance

1. Look in your dictionary. What does the person need to use or check?

   a. Turn left!   _turn signal_

   b. It's raining.   _____

   c. It's hot in here.   _____

   d. The battery needs recharging.   _____

   e. Do we need gas?   _____

   f. That car doesn't see us!   _____

   g. You're going too slow.   _____

   h. Stop at the next traffic light.   _____

   i. It's cold in here.   _____

   j. How fast are you going?   _____

   k. What's the weather report for tomorrow?   _____

   l. How many kilometres have we driven today?   _____

2. Look at the diagram of a rental car. An X shows a problem. Look at the list and check (✓) all the car parts that have problems.

   A&B Rental

   - ☐ brake light
   - ☑ bumper
   - ☐ headlight
   - ☐ hood
   - ☐ hubcap
   - ☐ licence plate
   - ☐ sideview mirror
   - ☐ tail light
   - ☐ tire
   - ☐ trunk
   - ☐ windshield

3. Label the car parts. Then match the parts with the problems. Write the number.

_2_ **a.** _____ tire _____

1. The car needs oil.

2. The tire needs air.

___ **b.** _____

3. The battery needs recharging.

___ **c.** _____

4. The car needs gas.

___ **d.** _____

5. The radiator needs coolant.

___ **e.** _____

4. What about you? Check (✓) the items you would like in a car.

☐ air bags   ☐ child safety seat   ☐ Other: _____

☐ air conditioning   ☐ stick shift   ☐ _____

☐ automatic transmission   ☐ tape deck   ☐ _____

Challenge Explain your choices in Exercise 4. Write sentences. **Example:** _I would like air conditioning because it's more comfortable._

An Airport

1. Look at the top picture in your dictionary. Answer the questions.

    a. How many passengers are in line at the check-in counter?   __2__

    b. What's the gate number?   _____

    c. What's the departure time?   _____

    d. How many children are near the boarding area?   _____

2. Circle the words to complete the sentences. Then write where the people are. Use the words in the box.

airline terminal	~~airplane~~	airplane
baggage claim area	cockpit	customs

Passenger: Where's your luggage?

Passenger: Up there. In the
    luggage carrier /(overhead compartment.)   __airplane__
        a.

Passenger: I feel nauseous.

Flight attendant: Here's an airsickness bag / oxygen mask.   _____
          b.

Passenger: I'm looking for the luggage from flight 371.

Airline rep: It will be on that carousel / helicopter.   _____
          c.

Passenger: Do you need help with that?

Passenger: No, thanks. I have a
    control tower / luggage carrier.   _____
        d.

Customs officer: Do you have anything to declare?

Passenger: Yes. Here's my declaration form / tray table.   _____
          e.

Pilot: This is your captain speaking. We will be at the
    check-in counter / gate in about seven minutes.   _____
        f.

Challenge Describe the airport in your dictionary. Write at least six sentences.

1. Look at page 111 in your dictionary. Complete the information for the passenger.

SKYAIR

Flight number:	508
Destination:	
Departure time:	
Seat number:	

2. Look in your dictionary. What is the passenger doing? Use the *-ing* form of the verb.

a. **Is this 14F?**   *finding his seat*

b. **Can I walk through now?**   _____

c. **Here's $100.**   _____

d. **There it is. Across the aisle.**   _____

e. **This is making me feel sick.**   _____

f. **Here it is! The large black one.**   _____

3. Look at the picture. Check (✓) the things the passenger did.

☑ got her boarding pass   ☐ stowed her carry-on bag   ☐ requested a pillow
☐ boarded the plane   ☐ fastened her seat belt   ☐ took off
☐ found her seat   ☐ looked at the emergency card   ☐ landed

Challenge List the things you can do to make a plane trip more comfortable. **Example:** *wear comfortable clothing*

▶ **Go to page 177 for Another Look (Unit 8).**

Types of Schools

1. Look in your dictionary. Where can you hear...?

   a. **It costs $10 000 a year.**   _____private school_____

   b. **I love playing with blocks.**   _____

   c. **How do you like U of T?**   _____

   d. **It looks like a church, Sister Mary.**   _____

   e. **Our parents' taxes pay for it.**   _____

   f. **That's the carburetor.**   _____

2. Match the typical student age with the school. You can use your dictionary for help.

   _2_ **a.** 20 years old   **1.** high school
   ___ **b.** 3 years old   **2.** college
   ___ **c.** 8 years old   **3.** preschool
   ___ **d.** 16 years old   **4.** middle school
   ___ **e.** 12 years old   **5.** elementary school
   ___ **f.** 30 years old   **6.** adult school

3. What about you? Complete the chart.

CHECK (✓) THE SCHOOLS YOU HAVE ATTENDED:	NAME	LOCATION	DATES
☐ elementary school			
☐ junior high school			
☐ high school			
☐ trade school			
☐ adult school			
☐ college/university			
☐ Other: _____			

Challenge Think of the different types of schools in another country. List in order the schools and the age of the typical student at each school.

112

1. Look in your dictionary. **True** or **False**?

    a. The writing assignment is due on October 3.   _____True_____

    b. The student is writing a first draft on his computer.   _____

    c. The student is editing his paper in red.   _____

    d. The student is getting feedback from another student.   _____

    e. The student is turning in his paper late.   _____

    f. The composition is about his job.   _____

    g. The final composition has more than one paragraph.   _____

2. Match the punctuation marks with the words. Write the number.

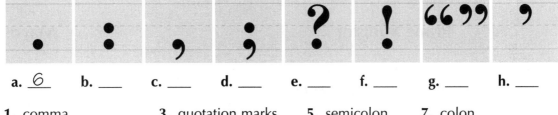

    a. _6_   **b.** ___   **c.** ___   **d.** ___   **e.** ___   **f.** ___   **g.** ___   **h.** ___

    1. comma   **3.** quotation marks   **5.** semicolon   **7.** colon

    2. exclamation mark   **4.** apostrophe   **6.** period   **8.** question mark

3. Look at the composition. Circle and correct four more punctuation mistakes.

> Name: Sonia Hernandez
>
> We're moving to San Diego;,California next
> September. Im worried. Will I like it? Where
> will we live. My father says, "Don't worry.'
> He says that I'll make new friends. My mother
> says that soon San Diego will feel like home.
> "But I'm happy here?" I exclaim. I watch my
> father's face and listen to my mother's words.
> I feel better.

4. What about you? How did you and your family feel the last time you moved? Write five sentences. Underline all the adjectives.

    Example: *I felt <u>excited</u>.*

Challenge Write a paper about your life in this country. Edit your paper. Get feedback. Rewrite your paper and turn it in to your teacher.

1. Look at the top of the page in your dictionary. Complete the chart with words under each heading.

Canadian Government		
Federal		**Municipal**
Parliament Buildings	Provincial Parliament Building	City Hall
	Provincial Parliament	
Prime Minister		Mayor

2. Look at the forms. Answer the questions.

Name: Hassan Al-Bahraini **Date of Birth:** 8/13/91	**Name:** Yoko Tanaka **Date of Birth:** 2/9/61
Address: 123 Main Street **Lived there** 8 years	**Address:** 64 Clark Rd. **Lived there** 1 year
Winnipeg, Manitoba	Lacombe, Alberta
Hassan Al-Bahraini 6/1/01	Yoko Tanaka 6/1/01
Signature **Date**	**Signature** **Date**

Name: Ana Suarez **Date of Birth:** 5/6/76	**Name:** Chen Lu **Date of Birth:** 11/11/86
Address: 35 Laurier Blvd. **Lived there** 10 years	**Address:** 11 Paul Rd. **Lived there** 2 years
Québec City, Québec	St. John, New Brunswick
Ana Suarez 6/1/01	Chen Lu 6/1/01
Signature **Date**	**Signature** **Date**

Who...?

a. has lived in Canada for three or more years   Hassan and Ana

b. is 18 years old or older   _____

c. can apply for Canadian Citizenship now?   _____

3. What about you? Have you ever...? Check (✓) **Yes** or **No**.

	YES	NO	IF YES, WHEN?
taken the Oath of Citizenship for Canada	☐	☐	_____
voted	☐	☐	_____
held a Canadian passport	☐	☐	_____
served on a jury	☐	☐	_____

Challenge Look at **page 184** in this book. Complete the information.

1. Look in your dictionary. Circle the events that happened first.

   a. Vikings reach Canada / French establish the first settlement.

   b. John Cabot reaches Canada / Jacques Cartier comes to Canada.

   c. Battle of the Plains of Abraham / War of 1812.

   d. Territory of Nunavut is established / Confederation is established.

   e. October Crisis in Québec / Red River Rebellion.

   f. Gold rush in British Columbia / Canadian Pacific Railway is completed.

   g. Canada celebrates its Centennial / Canada gets its own flag.

   h. Constitution and Charter of Rights signed / NAFTA agreement signed.

2. Look at the map. The provinces that united to form Canada in 1867 are shaded. Number the remaining provinces and territories in the order that they became part of Canada (Number 1 = the first province to join after 1867). Use your dictionary for help.

*Note: The borders of Ontario and Québec were different in 1867 than they are today.

3. Match the event to the year(s) it happened.

   a. __3__ Canada participates in World War I

   b. _____ Royal Colony of New France is founded

   c. _____ Internment of Japanese Canadians

   d. _____ Prime Minister Lester B. Pearson wins Nobel Peace Prize

   e. _____ Free Trade Agreement with United States of America

   f. _____ Statute of Westminster extends Canada's freedom from Britain

   1. 1663
   2. 1942
   3. 1914–1918
   4. 1931
   5. 1989
   6. 1957

4. Match the words with the pictures.

a. Canada's first prime minister, John A. Macdonald

b. _____

c. _____

d. _____

e. _____

f. _____

Mounties

the Canadarm

Canadian soldiers in
World War I

Chinese workers on the
Canadian Pacific Railroad

Centennial celebrations at
the Parliament buildings

Canada's first prime minister,
John A. Macdonald

Challenge What event in Canadian history would you like to know more about? Look it up in an encyclopedia or history book. Write a paragraph about it. Try to answer these questions. Who was there? When did it happen? Where did it happen? Why did it happen?

1. Look in your dictionary. Put the words in the correct category.

LAND		WATER
rain forest		

2. Complete the chart. Use words from Exercise 1.

a. largest	island		Greenland (Denmark)	2 175 600 sq. kilometres
b. highest	_____		Everest (Asia)	8848 metres
c. largest	_____		Sahara (N. Africa)	9 000 000 sq. kilometres
d. largest	_____		Arabia	2 149 690 sq. kilometres
e. largest	lake		Caspian Sea (Asia/Europe)	378 400 sq. kilometres
f. longest	_____		Nile (Africa)	6670 kilometres
g. deepest	_____		Pacific	10 924 metres
h. highest	_____		Angel (Venezuela)	807 metres

3. What about you? Check (✔) the places you've been to.

☐ waterfall   ☐ desert   ☐ ocean   ☐ Other: _____

Challenge Look at **pages 122 and 123** in your dictionary. Write the names of two islands, two oceans, two peninsulas, and two rivers. Do not use the ones from Exercise 2.

Mathematics

1. Look in your dictionary. Cross out the word that doesn't belong. Write the category.

a. <u>Operations</u>	addition	division	~~trigonometry~~	subtraction
b. _____	parallel	rectangle	circle	oval
c. _____	radius	angle	diameter	circumference
d. _____	geometry	algebra	calculus	multiplication
e. _____	square	cone	sphere	cylinder
f. _____	straight	perpendicular	pyramid	curved
g. _____	side	cube	diagonal	angle
h. _____	difference	quotient	algebra	product

2. Label the pictures. Use the words in the box.

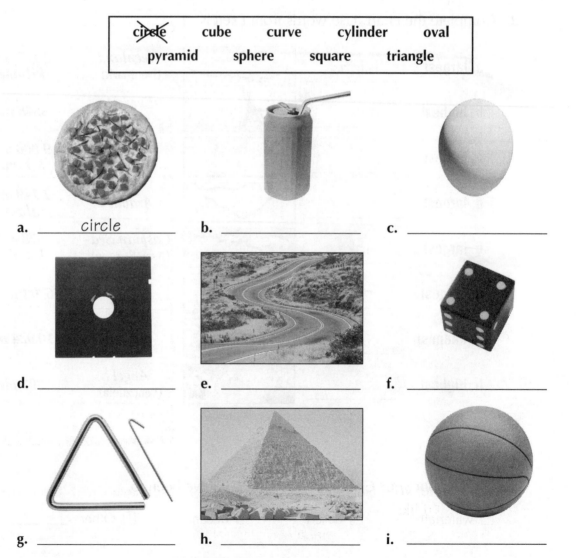

~~circle~~	cube	curve	cylinder	oval
pyramid	sphere	square	triangle	

a. ____<u>circle</u>____

b. _____

c. _____

d. _____

e. _____

f. _____

g. _____

h. _____

i. _____

Challenge Look at Excercise 2. Think of more examples of lines, shapes, solids, parts of a circle, and parts of a square. Make a list.

1. Look in your dictionary. **True** or **False**?

    a. The <u>biology</u> teacher is observing something through a microscope.   *True*

    b. The <u>physics</u> teacher is using a Bunsen burner.   _____

    c. The <u>chemistry</u> teacher is writing a formula on the board.   _____

    d. A molecule of water has <u>two</u> atoms.   _____

2. Write the words in the box in alphabetical order on the lab inventory. Then look at the lab table. How many items are there? Complete the inventory.

> crucible tongs   test tubes   funnels   ~~beakers~~   graduated cylinders
>
>   Bunsen burners   ~~balances~~   Petri dishes   slides
>
>   droppers   microscopes   magnets   dissection kits   forceps

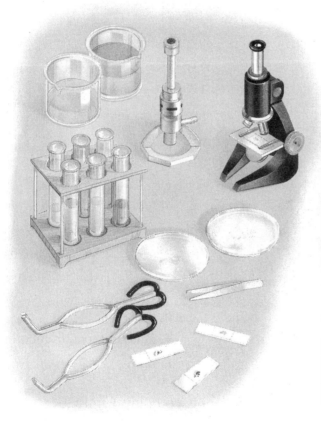

Lab Inventory

1.	*balances*	*0*
2.	*beakers*	*2*
3.		
4.		
5.		
6.		
7.		
8.		
9.		
10.		
11.		
12.		
13.		
14.		

3. What about you? Check (✔) the science classes you have taken. Circle the classes you would like to take.

    ☐ biology   ☐ chemistry   ☐ physics   ☐ Other: _____

Challenge   Change the <u>underlined</u> words in the false sentences in Exercise 1. Make the sentences true.

1. Look in your dictionary. Which instruments have…?

   a. strings   <u>violin</u>   <u>   </u>   <u>   </u>   <u>   </u>

   b. a keyboard   <u>piano</u>   <u>   </u>   <u>   </u>   <u>   </u>

2. Look at the bar graph. Number the instruments in order. (Number 1 = the instrument that the most people play)

Number of People Who Play Some of the Instruments in the Toronto Symphony Orchestra

   <u>   </u> **a.** clarinet   <u>   </u> **d.** drums

   <u>1</u> **b.** violin   <u>   </u> **e.** flute, trumpet, trombone

   <u>   </u> **c.** tuba, piano, harp   <u>   </u> **f.** horn

3. What about you? Check (✓) the instruments you play. Circle the instruments you would like to learn.

   ☐ piano   ☐ clarinet   ☐ flute

   ☐ guitar   ☐ drums   ☐ electric keyboard

   ☐ cello   ☐ Other: <u>   </u>

Challenge Find out about these instruments: viola, harmonica, harp, and bugle. What kinds of instruments are they? Look at the categories in your dictionary for help.

1. Look in your dictionary. In which class can you hear...?

a. [In 1996 the profit was higher.]   _economics_

b. [This sphere is easy to draw.]   _____

c. [Was ist das?]   _____

d. [Do you have that software program?]   _____

e. [What's the total?]   _____

f. [Tra-la-la-la-la. ♪♪♪]   _____

g. [Speak directly to the audience.]   _____

h. [Only five more sit-ups!]   _____

2. Look at the student's notes. Then complete the schedule with the words in the box.

TO DO THIS WEEK:
MON: Basketball practice
TUES: Take test on irregular verbs (buy-make)
WED: Make bookshelf
THURS: Bring disk and software
FRI: Sing Mozart's Requiem (auditorium)

choir	computer science
~~Phys. ed.~~	
English as a second language	
shop	

Mon.	Tues.	Wed.	Thurs.	Fri.
Phys.ed.				

3. What about you? Check (✓) the subjects you have taken. Circle the subjects you would like to take.

☐ art   ☐ business education   ☐ computer science

☐ economics   ☐ law   ☐ physical education

☐ shop   ☐ theatre arts   ☐ Other: _____

Challenge Find out which of the subjects in Exercise 3 you can take at your school.

1. Look in your dictionary. Answer the questions.

   a. Name seven American states that touch Canada.

     <u>New York</u>   _____   _____   _____

     _____   _____   _____

   b. Which parts of Canada are on Hudson Bay?

     _____   _____   _____   _____

   c. Which states in Mexico touch the United States?

     _____   _____   _____   _____

     _____

   d. Which countries in Central America are on the Pacific Ocean?

     _____   _____   _____   _____

     _____   _____

   e. Name four islands in the Caribbean Sea.

     _____   _____   _____   _____

2. Label the parts of Canada and the United States. You can use your dictionary for help.

In Canada:

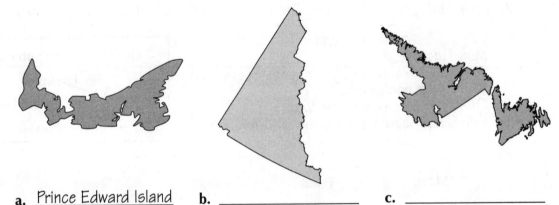

   a. <u>Prince Edward Island</u>   **b.** _____   **c.** _____

In the United States:

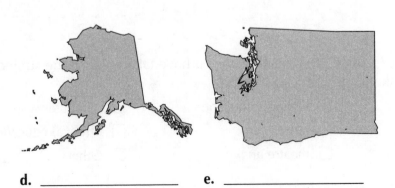

   d. _____   **e.** _____

3. Look in your dictionary. Circle the words to complete the sentences.

In Canada:

a. Alberta is (east)/ west of British Columbia.

b. The Yukon Territory is east / west of the Northwest Territories.

c. Nova Scotia is east / west of New Brunswick.

In the United States:

d. California is north / south of Oregon.

e. Idaho is north / south of Utah.

f. Wisconsin is east / west of Minnesota.

In Central America:

g. Nicaragua is north / south of Costa Rica.

h. Honduras is northeast / northwest of El Salvador.

i. Guatemala is southeast / southwest of Belize.

4. Match the state or province with the region and the country. Write a number and a letter for each item. You can use your dictionary for help.

	STATE OR PROVINCE	REGION	COUNTRY
5, A	**a.** Alberta	**1.** The Atlantic Provinces	**A.** Canada
_____	**b.** Campeche	**2.** The Midwest	**B.** Mexico
_____	**c.** Illinois	**3.** New England	**C.** The United States
_____	**d.** Massachusetts	**4.** The Pacific Northwest	
_____	**e.** Nova Scotia	**5.** The Prairie Provinces	
_____	**f.** Sonora	**6.** The Yucatan Peninsula	

5. What about you? Look at the map in your dictionary. Where have you visited? When were you there? Write sentences.

Example: *I drove to Nova Scotia in 1997.*

_____

_____

_____

_____

_____

_____

Challenge Imagine you are driving from Sydney, Nova Scotia to Whitehorse in the Yukon Territory. List in order the provinces you will drive through.

The World

1. Look in your dictionary. Cross out the country that doesn't belong.

   a. **North America**   Canada   United States   ~~Chile~~   Mexico
   b. **Asia**   China   Poland   India   Philippines
   c. **Europe**   Latvia   Ukraine   Belarus   Kazakhstan
   d. **Africa**   Namibia   Peru   Botswana   Sudan
   e. **South America**   Brazil   Paraguay   Guatemala   Colombia
   f. **Asia**   Syria   Iran   Saudi Arabia   Romania
   g. **Europe**   Greenland   France   Germany   Turkey

2. List the countries in the box in order of population size. (Number 1 = the most people) You can use your dictionary for help.

Argentina	Belarus	Iraq	Italy	Kenya	Mexico
	~~Pakistan~~		South Korea		

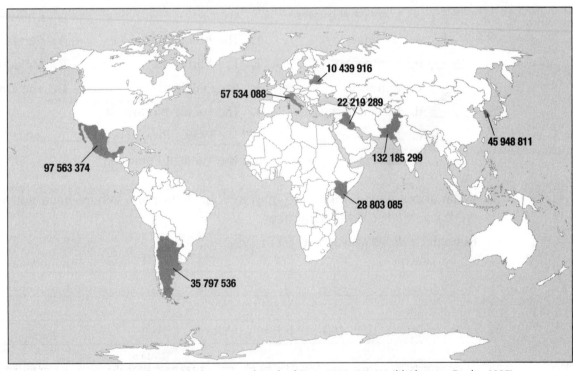

Based on information from: *The World Almanac and Book of Facts 1998.* (NJ: World Almanac Books, 1997)

1. _Pakistan_   3. _____   5. _____   7. _____
2. _____ 4. _____   6. _____   8. _____

3. Look in your dictionary. How many neighbours does … have? Write the names of the countries.

    a. In Europe:

    Romania   _5_   _Moldova, Bulgaria, Ukraine, Serbia, Hungary_

    b. In South America:

    Paraguay   ___   _____

    c. In Africa:

    Chad   ___   _____

    d. In Asia:

    Thailand   ___   _____

    e. In North America:

    Mexico   ___   _____

4. Match the oceans with their size. Write the number.

_3_ **a.** Indian

___ **b.** Atlantic

___ **c.** Arctic

___ **d.** Pacific

1. 73 427 000 square kilometres

2. 86 557 000 square kilometres

3. 9 485 000 square kilometres

4. 166 241 000 square kilometres

Based on information from: *The World Almanac and Book of Facts 1998.* (NJ: World Almanac Books, 1997)

5. What about you? Complete the information.

MY COUNTRY	CONTINENT	NUMBER OF NEIGHBOURS	POPULATION
_____	_____	_____	_____

Write the names of your country's neighbours.

_____

Challenge Look at **page 185** in this book. Complete the information.

1. Look in your dictionary. Which forms of energy come from...?

ATOMS

_____nuclear_____

THE EARTH

_____

_____

WATER

_____

AIR

_____

_____

THE SUN

_____

2. Match the newspaper headlines with the types of pollution. Write the letter.

BEACHES SAFE FOR SWIMMING THIS SUMMER

a.

Cars Get New Anti-Smog Device

b.

Farmers Stop Using Dangerous Chemicals On Grapes

c.

Countries Agree To Stop Making Atomic Bombs

d.

Petroco Cleans Up Water After Boating Accident

e.

Report Shows Hospitals More Careful With Medical Garbage

f.

__f__ **1.** hazardous waste

____ **2.** water pollution

____ **3.** oil spill

____ **4.** pesticide poisoning

____ **5.** radiation

____ **6.** air pollution

3. What are the people doing? Use the words in the box.

recycling	~~saving energy~~	saving energy	saving water

a. I always turn off the lights.

_____saving energy_____

b. I turn the tap off while I brush my teeth.

_____

c. I return cans and bottles to the store.

_____

d. I always use public transportation.

_____

4. What about you? Check (✓) the conservation steps you take. I....

☐ recycle   ☐ conserve water   ☐ conserve energy   ☐ Other: _____

Challenge Look at Exercise 3. List three other ways to conserve water or energy.

1. Look in your dictionary. **True** or **False**?

a. There are ten planets in our solar system. _____False_____

b. Saturn has rings. _____

c. The astronaut is looking through a telescope at the space station. _____

d. The astronomer is at an observatory. _____

e. There are six stars in the constellation. _____

2. Complete the chart with the names of the planets. Then answer the questions.

Which planet...?

a. is closest to the sun _____Mercury_____

b. is farthest from the sun _____

c. is the largest _____

d. has rings _____

e. is between Uranus and Pluto _____

f. is our home _____

3. What about you? What can you see in the night sky? Check (✓) **Yes** or **No**.

	YES	NO	
planets	☐	☐	If yes, which one(s)? _____
the moon	☐	☐	If yes, which phase? ☐ new ☐ full ☐ quarter ☐ crescent
stars	☐	☐	
constellations	☐	☐	
comets	☐	☐	

Challenge Find out the names of different constellations. What do they look like?

▶ **Go to page 178 for Another Look (Unit 9).**

Trees and Plants

1. Look in your dictionary. **True** or **False**?

    a. A tree has roots.   _____True_____

    b. Holly is a plant.   _____

    c. The birch tree has yellow leaves.   _____

    d. The magnolia and dogwood have pink flowers.   _____

    e. The cactus has a trunk.   _____

    f. Poison sumac has berries.   _____

    g. Poison ivy has needles.   _____

    h. The willow has cones.   _____

    i. The oak has branches and twigs.   _____

2. Look at the bar graph. Number the trees in order of height. (Number 1 = the tallest)

Based on information from: Petrides, G.: *Peterson Field Guides: Trees and Shrubs.* (NY: Houghton-Mifflin Co., 1986)

    ___ dogwood   ___ maple   ___ palm   _1_ Sitka spruce

    ___ elm   ___ oak   ___ pine   ___ willow

_____ **Challenge** Which trees grow near your home? Make a list.

1. Look in your dictionary. What colour is the…?

a. tulip   _____pink_____   **e.** gardenia   _____

b. daisy   _____   **f.** jasmine   _____

c. crocus   _____   **g.** daffodil   _____

d. poinsettia   _____   **h.** carnation   _____

2. Put the words in the box in the correct part of the diagram.

bud	bulb
leaf	petal
root	~~seed~~
stem	thorn

above the ground

seed

below the ground

3. Match the provinces with the flowers. Write the number. Look at **page 116** in your dictionary for help.

Some Canadian Provincial Flowers

____ **a.** British Columbia   **1.** wild rose

____ **b.** Ontario   **2.** white trillium

____ **c.** Alberta   **3.** pacific dogwood

____ **d.** Manitoba   **4.** mayflower

____ **e.** Nova Scotia   **5.** prairie crocus

4. What about you? Do you have flowers in your…? Check (✔) **Yes** or **No**.

	YES	NO	IF YES, WHAT KIND(S)?
home	☐	☐	_____
garden	☐	☐	_____

Challenge Find out the names of some other provincial and territorial flowers. Make a list.

Marine Life, Amphibians, and Reptiles

1. Look in your dictionary. Cross out the word that doesn't belong. Write the category.

   a. ___Reptiles___   turtle   alligator   ~~seal~~   crocodile

   b. _____   fin   gills   scales   scallop

   c. _____   shark   frog   toad   newt

   d. _____   sea lion   dolphin   lizard   otter

   e. _____   tuna   whale   shark   cod

2. Look at the chart. Circle the correct words to complete the sentences. You can use your dictionary for help.

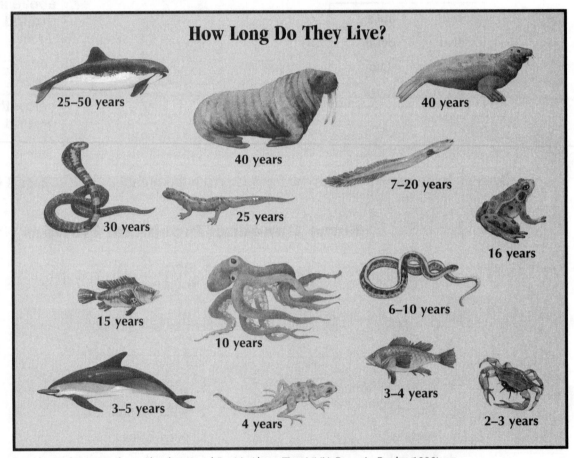

How Long Do They Live?

25–50 years

40 years

40 years

7–20 years

30 years

25 years

16 years

15 years

10 years

6–10 years

3–5 years

4 years

3–4 years

2–3 years

Based on information from: Shook, M. and R.: *It's About Time!* (NY: Penguin Books, 1992)

   a. The <u>frog /</u> (octopus) lives ten years.

   b. The <u>cod / bass</u> lives fifteen years.

   c. The <u>cobra / lizard</u> lives thirty years.

   d. The <u>porpoise / dolphin</u> only lives three to five years.

   e. The <u>eel / garter snake</u> can live to twenty years.

   f. The <u>crab / salamander</u> only lives a few years.

   g. The walrus and the <u>seal / dolphin</u> live forty years.

   h. The <u>cobra / garter snake</u> lives six to ten years.

3. Find and circle the 14 sea animal words. The words go → and ↓.

```
J  E  L  L  Y  F  I  S  H  O
O  E  I  A  E  I  N  Q  U  N
B  L  S  K  A  R  T  U  S  K
S  E  W  O  R  M  E  I  M  L
E  O  O  R  U  S  S  D  U  S
A  C  R  A  Y  E  T  I  S  H
H  T  D  O  G  R  U  N  S  A
O  O  F  L  O  U  N  D  E  R
R  P  I  G  S  N  A  I  L  K
S  U  S  H  I  O  R  N  K  E
E  S  H  R  I  M  P  A  L  M
```

4. What about you? Make two lists using the words from Exercise 3.

THINGS I EAT:

_____

_____

_____

_____

_____

THINGS I DON'T EAT:

_____

_____

_____

_____

_____

Challenge Add to your lists in Exercise 4. Use your dictionary for help.

Birds, Insects, and Arachnids

1. Look in your dictionary. Complete the chart.

	NAME OF BIRD	HABITAT*	PHYSICAL APPEARANCE
a.	robin	▨ ▨ ▨ ■	Brown with orange breast.
b.		▨ ▨	Blue with white on wings, head, and breast.
c.		■ ■	Large. Brown with white head and tail. Big yellow beak and claws.
d.		▨	Large head, flat face with big eyes. Brown and white feathers.
e.		■ ▨	Blue-black feathers with purple throat.
f.		▨ ▨	Green with red throat. Long, thin bill.
g.		■	Large. Long black neck and head. White "chin" and breast.
h.		▨	Black and white with small red spot on head. Small bill.
i.		■	Green head and neck. White neck "ring," brown chest and tail.
j.		■ ▨	Small. Brown, white and grey feathers.

*where the bird lives: ▨ = forests ■ = water ■ = mountains ▨ = farms ▨ = suburban gardens ■ = cities

2. Look at the picture. Check (✓) the insects in the garden.

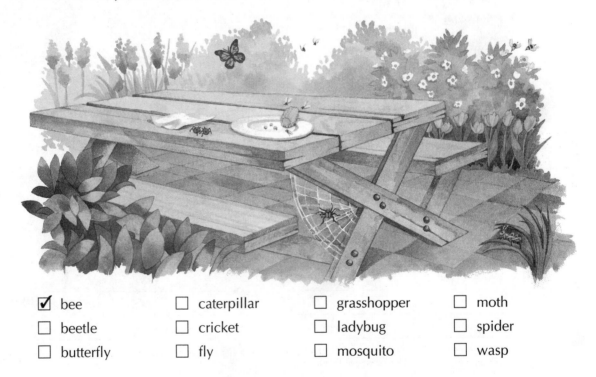

- ☑ bee
- ☐ beetle
- ☐ butterfly
- ☐ caterpillar
- ☐ cricket
- ☐ fly
- ☐ grasshopper
- ☐ ladybug
- ☐ mosquito
- ☐ moth
- ☐ spider
- ☐ wasp

3. What about you? Make a list of the birds and insects you can see near your home.

Challenge Which insects "help" people? Which insects cause problems for people?

Domestic Animals and Rodents

1. Look in your dictionary. Cross out the word that doesn't belong.

a. Pets	goldfish	guinea pig	~~squirrel~~	dog
b. Baby animals	sheep	puppy	kitten	baby chipmunk
c. Farm animals	horse	cow	groundhog	pig
d. Rodents	rat	mouse	chipmunk	goat
e. Birds	parakeet	donkey	rooster	hen

2. Check (✔) the animals that are on the list of the Top Ten Pets in North America.

- ☑ goldfish
- ☐ groundhog
- ☐ dog
- ☐ parakeet
- ☐ mouse
- ☐ snake
- ☐ cat
- ☐ pig
- ☐ guinea pig
- ☐ hamster
- ☐ rabbit
- ☐ chipmunk
- ☐ turtle
- ☐ ferret

Top Ten Pets

ferret

hamster

Based on information from: *The World Almanac for Kids 1997.* (NJ: World Almanac Books, 1996)

Challenge Survey your classmates. Find out if people have pets in their countries. Which ones are popular?

133

1. Look in your dictionary. **True** or **False**?

   a. The beaver lives in North America.   _____True_____

   b. The lion lives in North America.   _____

   c. The koala lives in Africa.   _____

   d. The elephant lives in Asia.   _____

   e. The llama lives in South America.   _____

2. Look at the photographs. Circle the correct words to complete the statements.

   a. The <u>antelope</u> / (deer) has <u>antlers</u> / <u>horns</u>.

   b. The <u>camel</u> / llama has a <u>hump</u> / <u>trunk</u>.

   c. The <u>bear</u> / <u>monkey</u> has a long <u>tail</u> / <u>neck</u>.

   d. The <u>elephant</u> / rhinoceros has <u>horns</u> / <u>tusks</u>.

   e. The <u>porcupine</u> / platypus has long, sharp <u>quills</u> / <u>whiskers</u>.

   f. The <u>lion</u> / <u>mountain lion</u> has four <u>hooves</u> / <u>paws</u>.

   g. The <u>kangaroo</u> / hyena has a <u>pouch</u> / <u>trunk</u>.

   h. The <u>skunk's</u> / <u>raccoon's</u> <u>coat</u> / mane is black and white.

3. Look at these endangered* mammals.

North America

China and Italy

Africa

Asia, Africa

Asia

China

Australia

Africa

South America

Asia

North America

Africa

Mongolia and China

North America

Based on information from the Fish and Wildlife Service, U.S. Department of the Interior, as of 1998.

*endangered = very few still living; they may not continue to live

Check (✓) the animals that are endangered.

☐ moose	☐ gorilla	☐ coyote	✔ grey bat
☐ red wolf	☐ fox	☐ camel	☐ leopard
☐ armadillo	☐ mountain lion	☐ hippopotamus	☐ elephant
☐ anteater	☐ tiger	☐ opossum	☐ panther
☐ panda	☐ zebra	☐ koala	☐ black rhinoceros
☐ giraffe	☐ brown bear	☐ buffalo	☐ kangaroo

Challenge Write a paragraph about one of the animals in your dictionary. Where does it live? What does it eat? How long does it live? Is it endangered?

▶ **Go to page 179 for Another Look (Unit 10).**

1. Look in your dictionary. Who said…?

a. We caught a lot of salmon today! commercial fisher

b. Do you want me to check the oil? _____

c. These roses are for the people in apartment 5-G. _____

d. This is the story of an elephant named Babar. _____

e. Mmm. This soup smells good! _____

f. You made $25 365.23 last year. _____

g. Our plane lands at 2:20 P.M. _____

2. Match the jobs with the tools. Write the number.

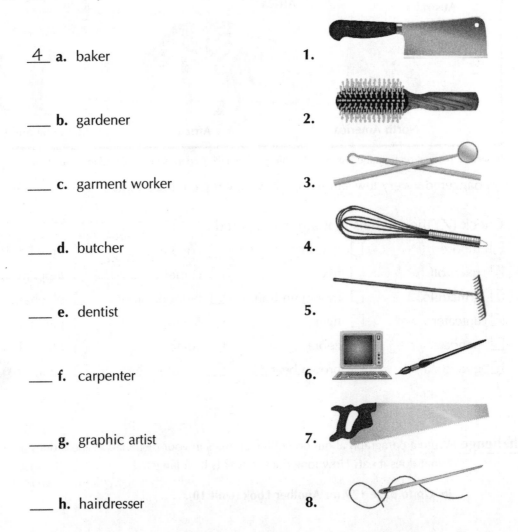

_4_ **a.** baker   1.

___ **b.** gardener   2.

___ **c.** garment worker 3.

___ **d.** butcher   4.

___ **e.** dentist   5.

___ **f.** carpenter   6.

___ **g.** graphic artist 7.

___ **h.** hairdresser   8.

3. Look in your dictionary. Put the jobs in the correct categories.

FOOD	CLOTHING	HEALTH	HOUSING
baker	_____	_____	_____
_____		_____	_____
_____		_____	_____
_____		_____	_____
_____			

4. Look at the bar graph.

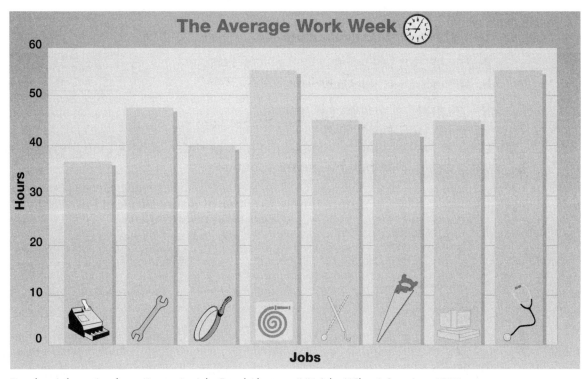

Based on information from: Krantz, L.: *Jobs Rated Almanac.* (NY: John Wiley & Sons Inc., 1995)

Who works…? Use the words in the box.

auto mechanic	carpenter	~~cashier~~	computer programmer
cook	dentist	doctor	firefighter

a. 37.5 hours a week   _____cashier_____

b. 40 hours a week   _____

c. 42.5 hours a week   _____

d. 45 hours a week   _____ and _____

e. 47.5 hours a week   _____

f. 55 hours a week   _____ and _____

Challenge Ask four people about their jobs. What do they do? How many hours a week do they work?
Example: *Meng is a cashier. She works 25 hours a week.*

1. Look in your dictionary. **True** or **False**? Put a question mark (**?**) if the information isn't there.

    a. The janitor is sweeping the floor.   <u>   False   </u>

    b. The interpreter can speak Spanish.   <u>   </u>

    c. The printer is using a computer.   <u>   </u>

    d. The machine operator is wearing safety glasses.   <u>   </u>

    e. The lawyer is in court.   <u>   </u>

    f. The movers are carrying a love seat.   <u>   </u>

    g. The nurse is taking the patient's blood pressure.   <u>   </u>

    h. The messenger rides a bicycle.   <u>   </u>

    i. The model is wearing a blue dress.   <u>   </u>

2. Look at the bar graph. Number the jobs in order of how many hours people work each week. (Number 1 = the most hours)

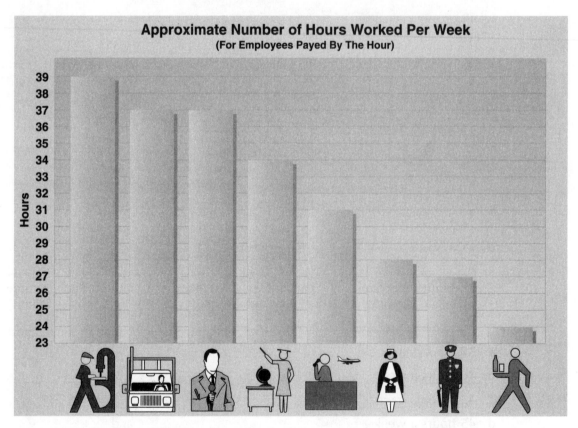

Approximate Number of Hours Worked Per Week
(For Employees Payed By The Hour)

Based on Statistics Canada: Catalogue Number 72F0002-XDE

   ____ a. travel agent   **_1_ e.** machine operator

   ____ b. server   **____ f.** truck driver

   ____ c. police officer   **____ g.** teacher/educator

   ____ d. reporter   **____ h.** nurse

3. Look in your dictionary. Circle the correct words to complete the sentences.

   a. The housekeeper / (nurse) is wearing a white hat.

   b. The student / teacher is pointing to a map.

   c. The messenger / postal worker is holding packages.

   d. The receptionist / secretary is speaking to a man.

   e. The stock clerk's / store owner's name is Kim.

   f. The salesclerk / telemarketer is on the phone.

   g. The reporter / writer is on television.

   h. The serviceman / welder is wearing a mask.

4. Look at the job preference chart. Choose the right person for the job.

LIKES TO...	ARI	LUISA	TOM	CHRIS	MIA	DAVE
work with people			✓	✓	✓	
speak on the phone	✓					
be inside	✓	✓		✓		
be outside		✓			✓	✓
sell things	✓					
explain ideas				✓		
speak languages			✓			
travel			✓		✓	
repair things		✓				
help people			✓	✓		
wear a uniform					✓	
do physical work					✓	✓

   a. telemarketer _____Ari_____   **d.** welder _____

   b. instructor _____   **e.** mover _____

   c. serviceman/servicewoman _____   **f.** interpreter _____

5. What about you? Look at **pages 136–139** in your dictionary. Write the jobs.

   Jobs I can do now: _____

   Jobs I can't do now: _____

   Jobs I would like to do: _____

   Jobs I wouldn't like to do: _____

Challenge Look at your answers in Exercise 5. Explain your choices.

Job Skills

1. Look in your dictionary. Circle the job skills in the employment ads below. Write the name of the job. Use the words in the box.

Assembler	Caregiver	Chef	~~Manager~~	Orderly
	Salesperson	Secretary	Server	

a.

_____Manager_____

wanted to (supervise) staff at our small, friendly architectural company.

Call 555-2544.

b.

_____

wanted to take care of small children. Must speak English and Spanish. Experience and references required. 555-3423

c.

_____

wanted to assist medical patients at the new Riverside Nursing Home. Good income. Experience required. Fax: 555-6545

d.

_____

needed to assemble telephone parts in midtown factory. Immediate full-time employment.

Call 555-2134.

e.

_____

needed to sell cars at our new Route 29 location. Must have experience and be able to work weekends. 555-0131

f.

_____

needed for busy law office. Must work on a computer and type 50 words per minute. 9:00–5:00.

555-0034

g.

_____

wanted to cook everything from hamburgers to duck l'orange at our small, neighbourhood restaurant. The Corner Bistro, 230 Park Street.

h.

_____

needed to wait on customers at a busy downtown coffee shop. Part-time only. Experience preferred.

555-1168

2. What about you? Check (✔) the job skills you have. Circle the skills you want to learn.

☐ drive a truck

☐ operate heavy machinery

☐ cook

☐ use a computer

☐ use a cash register

☐ supervise people

☐ speak another language

☐ repair appliances

☐ do manual labour

☐ Other: _____

Challenge Choose two job ads from Exercise 1. Can you do the jobs? Why or why not?

1. Look in your dictionary. Fill out Dan King's job application.

EJ'S MARKET　　　　　　　　　　　　**EMPLOYMENT APPLICATION**

Name: _Dan King_　　　　　　　　　　Job applying for: _____

1. How did you hear about this job? (Please check <u>all</u> appropriate boxes.)

　☐ friends　☐ classifieds　☐ school counsellor　☐ job board　☐ help wanted sign

2. Hours: ☐ part-time　☑ full-time

3. Have you had any experience? ☐ yes　☐ no　If yes, where? _____

4. References _Sam Parker, Manager, Shopmark Supermarket_ _____

- - - - - - - - - - - - - - - - - - **For Office Use Only** - - - - - - - - - - - - - - - - - -

Interviewed by: _Mr. Hill_ _____

Hired? ☐ yes　☐ no　Salary: _____

---

2. Match the job applicant's words with what she is doing. Write the number.

_3_ **a.** What's the starting pay?　　　**1.** She's asking about benefits.

___ **b.** Great. When can I start?　　　**2.** She's talking about her experience.

___ **c.** Hello. I saw your help-wanted ad. Is the job still available?　　　**3.** She's inquiring about the salary.

___ **d.** I worked at C.L. Thompson for two years.　　　**4.** She's getting hired.

___ **e.** What about vacation time?　　　**5.** She's calling for information.

3. What about you? What do you think are the best ways to find a job? Number them in order. (Number 1 = the best)

___ look in the classifieds　　___ look for a help wanted sign　　___ talk to friends

___ look at a job board　　___ Other: _____

Challenge Survey your classmates. How did they find their jobs?

An Office

1. Look at the top picture in your dictionary. Where's the paper? Circle the office items that have paper in or on them.

<u>typewriter</u>　　　　stapler　　　　　　swivel chair　　　　clipboard

desk pad　　　　　　stacking tray　　　　paper cutter　　　　postal scale

calculator　　　　　supply cabinet　　　fax machine　　　　paper shredder

2. Match the instructions with the office supplies. Write the number.

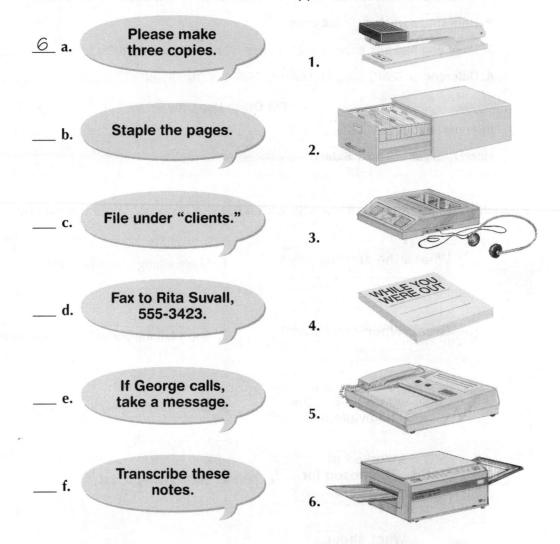

_6_ a. 　Please make three copies.

1.

___ b. 　Staple the pages.

2.

___ c. 　File under "clients."

3.

___ d. 　Fax to Rita Suvall, 555-3423.

4.

___ e. 　If George calls, take a message.

5.

___ f. 　Transcribe these notes.

6.

3. Look at the top picture in your dictionary. What can people use to find out...?

　a. how many stamps a letter needs　　　_postal scale_

　b. John Taylor's address　　　_____

　c. the answer to 1236 x 189　　　_____

　d. today's date　　　_____

4. Look at the supply cabinet. Complete the office inventory. You can use your dictionary for help.

Office Supplies

1 _____clipboard_____

6 bottles of _____

4 bottles of _____

2 bottles of _____

2 boxes of _____

3 boxes of _____

4 rolls of _____

5 rolls of _____

2 _____ pads

4 _____ pads

3 _____ pads

4 _____

2 _____

3 _____

1 bag of _____

5. What about you? How often do you…? Check (✓) the correct columns.

	OFTEN	SOMETIMES	NEVER
type a letter			
use a fax machine			
collate papers			
file papers			
use Post-it notes			
use a pencil sharpener			
use an organizer			
use a desk calendar			
Other: _____			

Challenge Look at **page 185** in this book and answer the questions.

Computers

1. Look in your dictionary. <u>Underline</u> the dictionary words that are in the ad.

Multimedia <u>Computer</u>

FREE PRINTER WITH PURCHASE!

- 166mhz Pentium Processor
- 32MB SDRAM Memory
- 512KB Pipeline Burst Cache
- 3.2GB Hard Drive
- 17LS Monitor (15.7")
- 12X CD-ROM Drive
- Internal 335 Fax Modem
- 16-bit Stereo Sound Card
- Speakers
- 101-key Space Saver Keyboard
- MF Mouse
- Pre-loaded Software

$2399

2. Complete the ad. Use the words in the box.

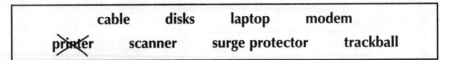

cable	disks	laptop	modem
~~printer~~	scanner	surge protector	trackball

a. laser _printer_ $202

b. _____ $28

c. _____ $239

d. _____ $199

e. 25 high density _____ $7.99

f. 280 mhz _____ $1699

g. 6' _____ $8.99

h. _____ $79.99

<u>Challenge</u> Find a computer ad. <u>Underline</u> the words you know.

1. Look in your dictionary. Who said...?

a. Your dinner is here.   room service

b. I'm making the bed now. _____

c. That's $3.00, sir. _____

d. Please take the Smiths' luggage to room 365, Carl. _____

e. I'll put my clothes in the dresser. _____

f. You're in room 636, Ms. Jones. _____

2. Look at the guest room hotel directory. What number do you call for...?

Hotel Edison

a. room service   3
b. gift shop   —
c. pool   —
d. meeting room   —
e. front desk   —
f. housekeeper   —
g. bellhop   —

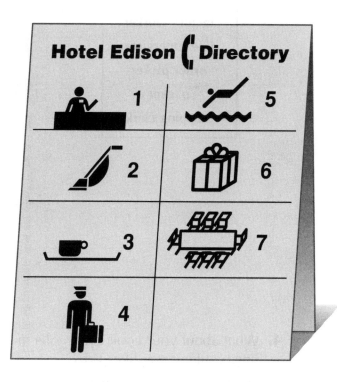

Hotel Edison Directory

1   5
2   6
3   7
4

3. What about you? Would you like to be a guest at the hotel shown in your dictionary? Check (✓) **Yes** or **No**.

☐ Yes   ☐ No   Why? _____

Challenge Look in your dictionary. Write five questions that you can ask the desk clerk about the hotel.
     Example: *What time is the pool open?*

A Factory

1. Look in your dictionary. **True** or **False**?

   a. The factory manufactures lamps. _____True_____

   b. The factory owner is in the warehouse. _____

   c. The time clock is near the designer's office. _____

   d. The line supervisor and packer have clipboards. _____

   e. There are three boxes on the hand truck. _____

2. Cross out the word that doesn't belong.

a. People	designer	shipping clerk	~~forklift~~	packer
b. Places	time clock	warehouse	front office	loading dock
c. Machines	hand truck	order picker	forklift	conveyor belt
d. Things workers do	ship	design	manufacture	parts

3. Read the descriptions. Write the names of the jobs. Use the words in the box.

   > ~~designer~~
   > factory worker
   > line supervisor
   > order picker
   > packer
   > shipping clerk

   Lamplighter, Inc.

   a. design the lamp _____designer_____

   b. watch the assembly line _____

   c. put together parts on the assembly line _____

   d. count boxes on the loading dock _____

   e. take boxes off the warehouse shelves _____

   f. put lamps in boxes on the conveyor belt _____

4. What about you? Look at the jobs in Exercise 3. Which one would you like? Which one wouldn't you like? Why?

   Example: *I would like to be a line supervisor. I like to supervise people.*

   _____

   _____

Challenge Rewrite the false sentences in Exercise 1. Make them true.

146

1. Look at **pages 136–139** in your dictionary. Who is wearing…?

    a. a hard hat   _____engineer_____ and _____

    b. latex gloves   _____ and _____

    c. safety glasses   _____

    d. a back support   _____

2. Label the safety symbols. Use the words in the box.

caution explosive	caution corrosive	danger poison	warning flammable	~~warning poison~~	danger flammable

    a. _____warning poison_____   **b.** _____   **c.** _____

    d. _____   **e.** _____   **f.** _____

    Note: The more sides the frame has, the more dangerous the product is.

3. Match the hazard words with these situations. Write the letter.

    _b_ **1.**   ___ **2.**   ___ **3.**

    ___ **4.**

    a. poison
    b. corrosive
    c. flammable
    d. explosive

4. Cross out the word that doesn't belong. Write the part of the body.

    a. _____ears_____   safety earmuffs   ~~respirator~~   earplugs

    b. _____   hair net   back support   hard hat

    c. _____   fire extinguisher   safety goggles   safety visor

    d. _____   safety vest   toe guard   safety boot

5. What about you? Do you use any of the items in Exercise 4? Check (✔) **Yes** or **No**.

    ☐ Yes   ☐ No   If yes, which ones? _____

Challenge   Which safety measures do you take at work? at home? Write a list for each.

Farming and Ranching

1. Look in your dictionary. Where can you find…? Write the locations.

a. oranges   in the   *orchard*

b. chickens   in front of the _____

c. farmworkers   in the _____

d. grapes   in the _____

e. cattle   in and near the _____

f. the rancher   on the _____

2. Look at the bar graph. Number the crops in order. (Number 1 = the biggest crop)

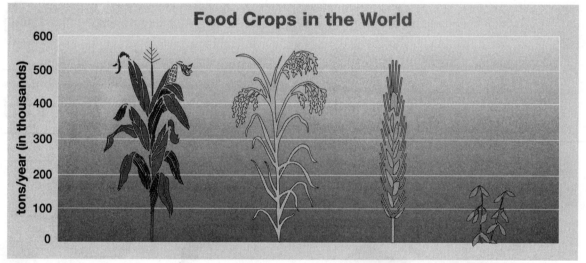

Food Crops in the World

tons/year (in thousands)

600
500
400
300
200
100
0

Based on information from: Ash, R.: *The Top Ten of Everything 1997.* (NY: DK Publishing Inc., 1996)

____ **a.** wheat   _1_ **b.** corn   ____ **c.** rice   ____ **d.** soybeans

3. What about you? Have you ever been…? Check (✔) **Yes** or **No**.

	YES	NO	IF YES, WHERE?
a. in a field	☐	☐	_____
b. in an orchard	☐	☐	_____
c. on a tractor	☐	☐	_____
d. in a barn	☐	☐	_____
e. in a vineyard	☐	☐	_____
f. on a farm	☐	☐	_____
g. on a ranch	☐	☐	_____
h. in a corral	☐	☐	_____
i. in a vegetable garden	☐	☐	_____

Challenge List products that come from wheat, soybeans, corn, cotton, and cattle.

1. Look in your dictionary. Put the words in the correct category.

HEAVY MACHINES	TOOLS	BUILDING MATERIAL
cherry picker	jackhammer	concrete
_____	_____	_____
_____	_____	_____
_____	_____	_____
	_____	_____
		_____
		_____
		_____
		_____

2. Match the jobs with the tools that the construction workers need. Write the number.

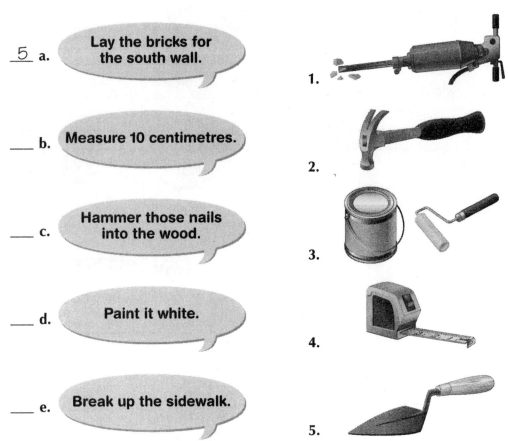

_5_ **a.** Lay the bricks for the south wall.

___ **b.** Measure 10 centimetres.

___ **c.** Hammer those nails into the wood.

___ **d.** Paint it white.

___ **e.** Break up the sidewalk.

1.

2.

3.

4.

5.

Challenge Look in your dictionary. What are the construction workers doing? Write sentences.
Example: *One construction worker is using a jackhammer.*

Tools and Building Supplies

1. Look in your dictionary. Cross out the word that doesn't belong.

a. Hardware	nail	bolt	~~outlet~~	screw
b. Plumbing	axe	plunger	pipe	fittings
c. Power tools	circular saw	hammer	router	electric drill
d. Paint	brush	roller	spray gun	chisel
e. Electrical	wire stripper	drill bit	wire	extension cord
f. Hand tools	hacksaw	flashlight	wrench	mallet

2. Look at the pictures. What do you need? Choose the correct tool from the box.

battery	drill bit	~~electrical tape~~	level
Phillips screwdriver	sandpaper	scraper	screwdriver

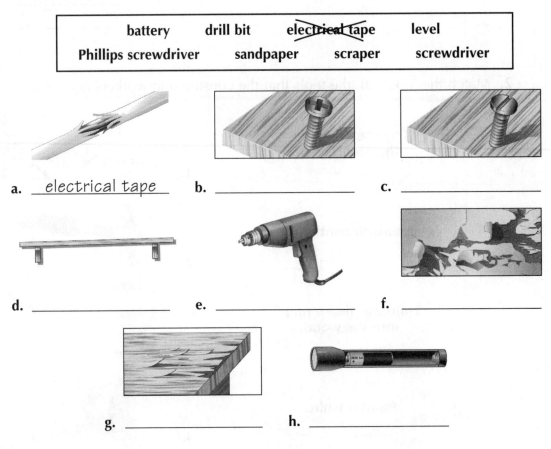

a. <u>electrical tape</u>   b. _____   c. _____

d. _____   e. _____   f. _____

g. _____   h. _____

3. Look at the picture. How many … are there?

a. nuts _6_   c. screws ___   e. bolts ___

b. nails ___   d. washers ___   f. hooks ___

4. Look at the chart.

Pocket Tool Features

Model	⬚	⬚	⬚	⬚	⬚	⬚	⬚
Deluxe	•	•	•	•	•	•	•
Traditional	•	•	•		•	•	
Micro	•				•		•

True or **False**?

a. All three models have screwdrivers.   _____True_____

b. The "Micro" has a Phillips screwdriver.   _____

c. The "Traditional" has a saw blade.   _____

d. The "Micro" has a straight blade.   _____

e. All three models have a tape measure.   _____

f. Only the "Deluxe" has a wire stripper.   _____

g. The "Deluxe" has pliers.   _____

5. What about you? Check (✔) the tools you have.

☐ hammer   ☐ plunger

☐ handsaw   ☐ level

☐ power sander   ☐ axe

☐ electric drill   ☐ circular saw

☐ wrench   ☐ Phillips screwdriver

☐ mallet   ☐ plane

☐ hacksaw   ☐ chisel

☐ screwdriver   ☐ Other: _____

Challenge Look at the chart in Exercise 4. Which model would you buy? What can you use it for?

▶ **Go to page 180 for Another Look (Unit 11).**

Places to Go

1. Look in your dictionary. Who said...?

a. **I'm cutting the hedges.**   <u>gardener</u>

b. **And the score is: the Reds 6 and the Comets 4.**   _____

c. **I'm going to feed the elephants.**   _____

2. Look in your dictionary. Circle all the dictionary words in the newspaper listing below.

What's Happening

Art
Newport (Art Gallery) special exhibit of paintings by local artists. Through August 15. $4

Children
The Purple Players puppet show, Crown Amusement Park. Weekends, 2:00–3:00. Free.
Town Square Annual Street Carnival. August 2–8, 10:00–8:00. Free.

Sports
Reds v. Kings baseball game, Hunter Field. August 11, 2:00. General admission: $2, Reserved seats: $4

General Interest
Union Square Flea Market, 10:00–6:00, every Sunday. Free.
Tiverton County Fair. Food, exhibitions, prizes. Admission: $5.50 adults, $3.00 kids.
Brosky Park Zoo, Elmwood Avenue. Special reptile exhibit until September 25. General admission: $5.00 adults, $2.50 children and senior citizens, free under 3.
Charles W. Smith Botanical Gardens. Flowers of every variety and colour. Free.

At the Movies
Independence Day (***PG-13) Will Smith, Bill Pullman, Apple Valley: 12:45, 3:45, 7:00
Jack (**PG-13) Robin Williams, Fran Drescher, Castle: 12:45, 2:45

3. Where can you go to...? Use the circled words from Exercise 2.

a. see animals   <u>zoo</u>

b. watch pictures on a screen   _____

c. look at sculpture   _____

d. sit in a stadium   _____

e. buy merchandise at a booth   _____

f. go on small rides and play games   _____

g. see greenhouse flowers   _____

h. ride a big roller coaster   _____

4. What about you? Where would you like to go next weekend? Why?

_____

Challenge Look in a local newspaper or at the listing in Exercise 2. Talk to two classmates and agree on a place to go. Write your decision and give a reason.

1. Look in your dictionary. Where can you…?

   a. have a picnic   at the _____picnic table_____

   b. play baseball   on the _____

   c. ride a bicycle   on the _____

   d. get a drink   at the _____

2. Look at the park map. Complete the legend. Use the words in the box.

ball field	**bike path**	**duck pond**	**picnic table**
playground	~~**tennis court**~~	**water fountain**	

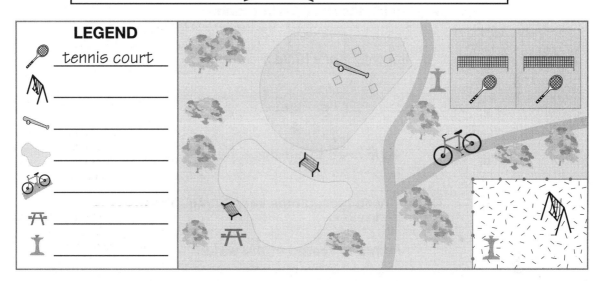

   LEGEND

   tennis court

   _____

   _____

   _____

   _____

   _____

   _____

3. Look at the map in Exercise 2. **True** or **False**?

   a. There's a water fountain in the playground.   _____True_____

   b. The tennis court is to the left of the ball field.   _____

   c. There's a seesaw in the playground.   _____

   d. There are benches near the duck pond.   _____

   e. The bike path goes around the duck pond.   _____

4. What about you? What did you do when you were a child? Check (✓) the boxes.

   ☐ ride a tricycle   ☐ picnic in the park   ☐ play on swings

   ☐ climb on the bars   ☐ play in the sandbox   ☐ go down the slide

   ☐ Other: _____

Challenge   Go to a neighbourhood park or look at the park in your dictionary. What are the people doing? Write eight sentences. **Example:** *A little girl is riding a tricycle.*

Outdoor Recreation

1. Look in your dictionary. How many people are…?

   a. hiking ___2___   d. camping ___   g. rafting ___

   b. mountain biking ___   e. fishing ___   h. backpacking ___

   c. canoeing ___   f. horseback riding ___   i. boating ___

2. Read the situations. What do the people need? Use the words in the box.

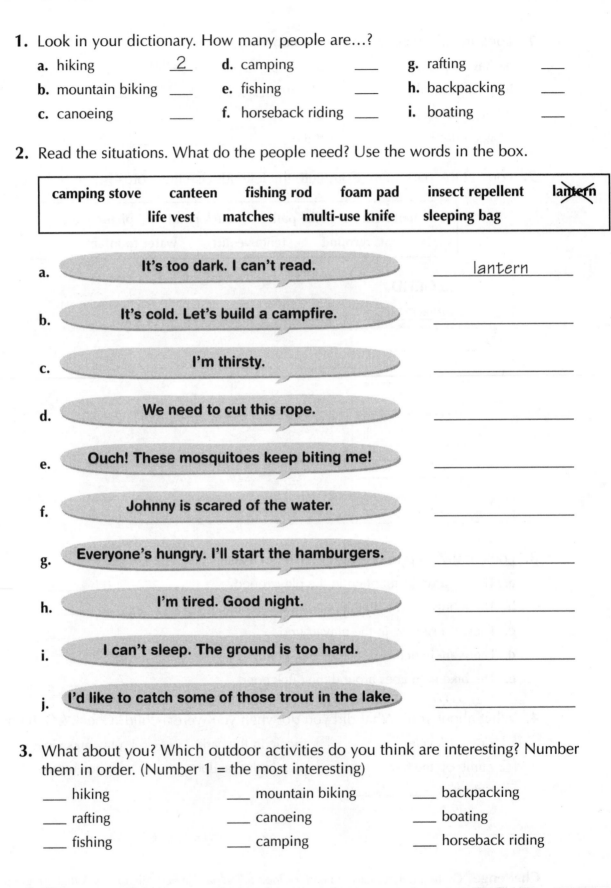

| camping stove | canteen | fishing rod | foam pad | insect repellent | ~~lantern~~ |
| life vest | matches | multi-use knife | sleeping bag |

a. It's too dark. I can't read.   lantern

b. It's cold. Let's build a campfire.   _____

c. I'm thirsty.   _____

d. We need to cut this rope.   _____

e. Ouch! These mosquitoes keep biting me!   _____

f. Johnny is scared of the water.   _____

g. Everyone's hungry. I'll start the hamburgers.   _____

h. I'm tired. Good night.   _____

i. I can't sleep. The ground is too hard.   _____

j. I'd like to catch some of those trout in the lake.   _____

3. What about you? Which outdoor activities do you think are interesting? Number them in order. (Number 1 = the most interesting)

   ___ hiking   ___ mountain biking   ___ backpacking

   ___ rafting   ___ canoeing   ___ boating

   ___ fishing   ___ camping   ___ horseback riding

Challenge Look at Exercise 3. List the things you need for your number 1 activity.

1. Look in your dictionary. What are the people using to...?

    a. build a sand castle   <u>sand</u>

    b. sit on the sand   _____ and _____

    c. keep drinks and food cold   _____

    d. protect their skin from the sun   _____ and _____

    e. stay warm in the water   _____

    f. breathe under the water   _____

2. Look at the chart. **True** or **False**?

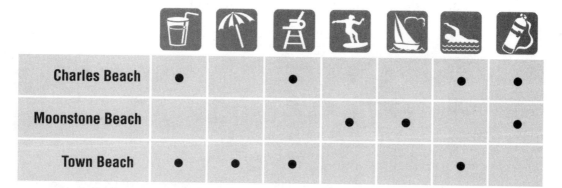

    a. You can swim at Charles Beach.   <u>True</u>

    b. You can use your surfboard only at Moonstone Beach.   _____

    c. You can go out in your sailboat at Town Beach.   _____

    d. You can use your scuba tank at Charles Beach.   _____

    e. You can rent a beach umbrella at Moonstone Beach.   _____

    f. There's a lifeguard at all three beaches.   _____

3. What about you? How important are these things to you? Circle the number.

	VERY IMPORTANT				NOT IMPORTANT
clean sand	4	3	2	1	0
high waves	4	3	2	1	0
shade	4	3	2	1	0
seashells	4	3	2	1	0
lifeguard station	4	3	2	1	0
Other: _____	4	3	2	1	0

Challenge   Look at the chart in Exercise 2. Which beach would you like? Why?

1. Look in your dictionary. Match the verbs with the sports. Write the number.

_5_ **a.** hit
___ **b.** swing
___ **c.** kick
___ **d.** shoot
___ **e.** ride

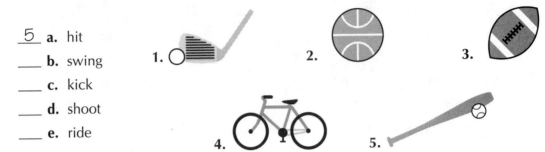

1. 2. 3.

4. 5.

2. Look at the bar graph. Complete the sentences.

Calories Burned per Hour

Based on information from Sutcliffe, A. (Editor): _Numbers: How Many, How Far, How Long, How Much._ (NY: HarperCollins, 1996)

a. When you _____jog_____, you burn 550 calories an hour.

b. When you _____, you burn 420 calories an hour.

c. When you _____, you burn 300 calories an hour.

d. When you _____, you burn 520 calories an hour.

e. When you _____, you burn 780 calories an hour.

f. When you _____, you burn 460 calories an hour.

g. When you _____, you burn 480 calories an hour.

Note: 1 kilojoule = 4.2 calories, for metric conversions.

3. Unscramble the sentences. Then look in your dictionary. **True** or **False**?

a. women in running Two are the park

    Two women are running in the park.   False

b. dribbling A is man the ball

c. is woman A stretching

d. into ocean diving A the is girl

e. A men tackling is man two

f. men are Three racing

g. man pitching is A a ball

4. Complete the analogies. Use the words in the box.

bend	finish	kick	pitch	serve	~~swim~~

a. ski : snow = _____ swim _____ : water

b. throw : catch = start : _____

c. catch : hands = _____ : feet

d. shoot : basketball = _____ : baseball

e. shoot : arms = _____ : waist

f. swing : golf = _____ : tennis

5. What about you? Check (✔) the correct boxes.

HOW OFTEN DO YOU...?	OFTEN	SOMETIMES	NEVER	WHERE?
work out	☐	☐	☐	_____
dive	☐	☐	☐	_____
skate	☐	☐	☐	_____
ski	☐	☐	☐	_____
race	☐	☐	☐	_____
swim	☐	☐	☐	_____
Other: _____	☐	☐	☐	_____
_____	☐	☐	☐	_____

Challenge Rewrite the false sentences in Exercise 3. Make them true.

Team Sports

1. Look at the hockey rink at the top of your dictionary page. Write the numbers.

   a. How many teams are there?   __2__

   b. How many players can you see?   _____

   c. How many goalies can you see?   _____

   d. How many defence players are on each team?   _____

   e. How many referees are there?   _____

   f. What's the score?   _____

2. Write the name of the sport. Use the words in the box. You can use your dictionary for help.

baseball	basketball	~~football~~
	soccer volleyball	

   a. __football__   b. _____   c. _____

   d. _____   e. _____

3. What about you? Circle the sports you have played. <u>Underline</u> the sports you have watched. Put a star (*) next to the sports you are a fan of.

softball	football	basketball	baseball
volleyball	hockey	curling	soccer

_____ **Challenge** How many players are there on a … team? If you don't know, try to find out.

basketball _____	baseball _____	football _____
soccer _____	hockey _____	volleyball _____

1. Look in your dictionary. In which sports do you...?

HIT A BALL	RIDE	THROW SOMETHING
billiards		
	LIFT SOMETHING	USE A TARGET
STAND ON WHEELS	WEAR A MASK	WEAR A LEOTARD

2. Look at the chart. List the sports in order of popularity. (Number 1 = the most popular)

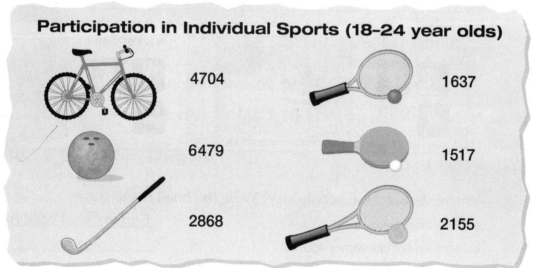

Participation in Individual Sports (18–24 year olds)

4704   1637

6479   1517

2868   2155

Based on information from The National Sporting Goods Association, 1994. (based on survey of 10 000 homes)

1.   bowling
2. _____
3. _____
4. _____
5. _____
6. _____

3. What about you? List three individual sports you participate in. (Number 1= the sport you do most often)

1. _____ 2. _____ 3. _____

Challenge   Interview at least four people. Which individual sports do they do? Make a list.
       Example: *Two students do weightlifting.*

1. Look in your dictionary. Circle the correct words to complete the sentences.

   a. The woman in the brown cap is (cross-country skiing) / downhill skiing.

   b. Two people are snowboarding / sledding.

   c. A woman in a red bathing suit is wind surfing / sailing.

   d. A man and woman are scuba diving / snorkelling.

2. Look at the hotel information.

Where should these people stay? Write the hotel name(s).

   a. Ana likes water sports.   _Caribe Plaza or Mirror Lake Inn_

   b. Mei-Yuan likes winter sports.   _____

   c. Jason loves downhill skiing.   _____

   d. Crystal wants to go snorkelling.   _____

   e. Paulo wants to take his children sledding.   _____

   f. Kyle wants to go sailing and waterskiing.   _____

   g. Olga wants to go surfing.   _____

   h. Taro loves sailing and sailboarding.   _____

3. What about you? Look at the hotels in Exercise 2. Where would you like to stay? Why?

   Example: *I'd like to stay at the Wicker Inn or at the Hillside Lodge. I like skating.*

Challenge Interview two people. Ask them which winter sports or water sports they like. Then recommend a hotel from Exercise 2.

1. Look in your dictionary. What do you see? Put the words in the box in the correct column.

arrow	~~bat~~	boots	bow	catcher's mask
club	glove	helmet	poles	racquet
inline skates	shin guards	shoulder pads	target	uniform

BASEBALL	FOOTBALL	SKIING	ARCHERY
bat			
_____	_____	_____	_____
_____			_____
_____			

GOLF	TENNIS	SKATING	SOCCER
_____	_____	_____	_____

2. Look at the chart. Complete the list.

On an average day, sports players buy...

3014   6153   8493   6619   33973

Based on information from: Heymann, T.: *On an Average Day.* (NY: Ballantine Books, 1989)

a. 8493   _basketballs_   **d.** 6619   _____

b. 3014   _____   **e.** 33 973 sets of   _____

c. 6153   _____

3. What about you? Check (✔) the sports equipment you have used.

☐ bowling ball   ☐ football   ☐ ice skates   ☐ flying disc   ☐ baseball
☐ snowboard   ☐ skis   ☐ volleyball   ☐ weights   ☐ Other: _____

Challenge   Look at **page 158** in your dictionary. Which sports equipment do you see? Make a list. You have only three minutes!

Hobbies and Games

1. Look in your dictionary. Cross out the word that doesn't belong.

   a. **Types of paint**   ~~clay~~   acrylic   oil   watercolour
   b. **Things to collect**   baseball cards   clubs   stamps   coins
   c. **Cards**   hearts   diamonds   spades   figurines
   d. **Games**   cards   checkers   crochet   chess
   e. **Kits**   doll making   woodworking   model   dice
   f. **Painting**   brush   canvas   glue   easel

2. Ask your classmates what hobbies they have. Fill in the chart.

HOBBY	NUMBER OF STUDENTS
collect something	
make something	
photography	
play games	
play cards	
watch videos / movies	
build models	
sew / knit	
cook	
other	

3. What about you? Look at the hobbies in Exercise 2. Write them in the correct column.

   HOBBIES I DO   **HOBBIES I DON'T DO**   **HOBBIES I WOULD LIKE TO DO**

   _____   _____   _____

   _____   _____   _____

   _____   _____   _____

   _____   _____   _____

4. Unscramble these hobby and game words. You can use your dictionary for help.

a. RODAB MAGE   (B) O A R D   G A M (E)

b. DIVOE MAGE   __ __ O__ __ __   __ __ O __

c. RANY   __ __ O __

d. GINFURIE   __ __ __ __ __ O __ __

e. PREPA LOLD   __ __ __ __ O __ O __ __

f. LACY   __ __ __ O

g. GRARTIDEC   __ __ __ __ __ __ __ O

Write the letters in the circles.   (B) ○ ○ ○ ○ ○ ○ ○ ○ ○

Unscramble the letters in the circles.

A hobby: __ __ __ __ __ __ __ __ __

5. What is it? Use unscrambled words from Exercise 4 to write what the people are talking about.

a. I'm putting this dress on *her.*

_____paper doll_____

b. I'm going to make a bowl with *it.*

_____

c. Checkers is my favourite *one.*

_____

d. I'm using *it* to knit a sweater.

_____

6. What about you? How much do you like to…? Check (✔) the correct columns.

	I LOVE IT	I LIKE IT	IT'S OK	I DON'T LIKE IT	I DON'T KNOW
paint					
do crafts					
play cards					
collect things					
play board games					
Other: _____					

Challenge   Look at **page 185** in this book. Complete the chart.

Electronics and Photography

1. Look in your dictionary. Circle the correct words to complete the sentences.

a. A (microphone) / remote control comes with the cassette recorder.

b. The portable TV is to the left / right of the large television.

c. The CD player is above / below the tuner.

d. The clock radio is above / below the shortwave radio.

e. The videocassette is inside / on the VCR.

f. The young man is wearing earmuffs / headphones.

g. The battery pack is to the left / right of the battery charger.

h. The slide tray is on / next to the carousel slide projector.

i. The video camera / 35 mm camera is to the left of the tripod.

2. Look at the ad. How much money can you save? Write the amount.

a. speakers $27.00   e. portable radio-cassette player _____

b. personal radio-cassette player _____   f. cassette recorder   _____

c. CD player   _____   g. 35 mm camera   _____

d. camcorder   _____   h. turntable   _____

3. Look at the control buttons. Write the function. Use the words in the box.

fast forward	pause	play	record	~~rewind~~	stop

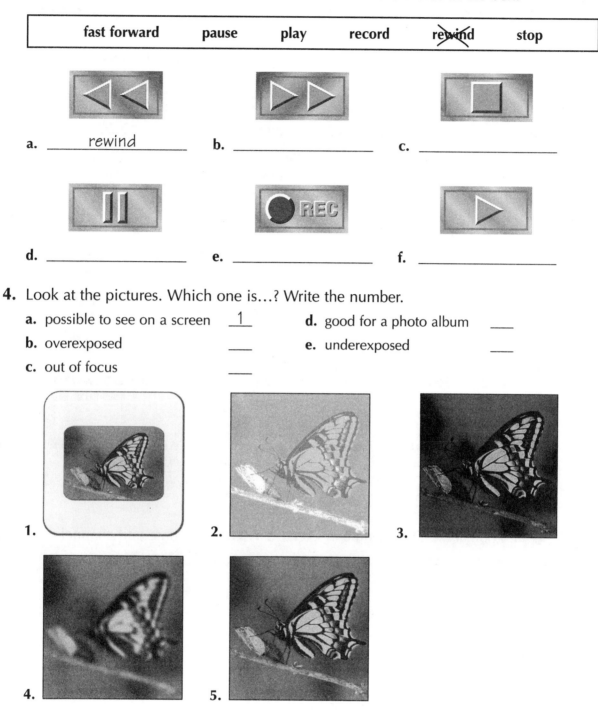

a. _____rewind_____   b. _____   c. _____

d. _____   e. _____   f. _____

4. Look at the pictures. Which one is…? Write the number.

a. possible to see on a screen __1__   d. good for a photo album ___

b. overexposed   ___   e. underexposed   ___

c. out of focus   ___

1.   **2.**   **3.**

4.   **5.**

5. What about you? Look at the ad in Exercise 2. Which item would you like to buy? Why?

_____

Challenge Find out today's prices for three of the items in Exercise 2. Compare the prices with the prices in the ad.

Entertainment

1. Look in your dictionary. Circle all the dictionary words in the TV schedule.

	8:00	**8:30**	**9:00**	**9:30**	**10:00**	**10:30**	**11:00**
2	**Entertainment Now** Stand-up comedy from L.A. clubs.	**Lisa!** Talk show host interviews soap opera stars.	**Movie:** Home Alone (1990 comedy). Family accidentally goes on vacation without 8-year-old son (Macaulay Culkin). Watch, but don't try it! ****				**News**
4	**Movie:** Mission Impossible (1996 action-adventure). Based on the popular television program. With Tom Cruise. ****				**Great Performances:** Bizet's opera Carmen. Performed live from Lincoln Center.		
5	**Wild World** Nature program looks at life in the jungle.	**Mystery!** Murder in a small town.			**The Twilight Zone** Visitors from Mars.		**News**
6	**Movie:** Marty (1955). Two lonely people find romance. Based on the play by Paddy Chayefsky.****			**How Things Work** A look inside the brain.	**Encore!** The New York City Ballet performs the Nutcracker Suite.		
7	**Time's Up!** New game show.	**The Simpsons** Cartoon.	**Movie:** Jaws (1975 horror). A large shark terrorizes tourists at a local beach. Directed by Steven Spielberg.*****				

The "SATURDAY EVENING" banner appears above the schedule.

2. Look at the TV schedule in Exercise 1. Write the time and channel if you want to....

   a. laugh at funny stories   <u>8:00, Channel 2</u>

   b. watch dancing   _____

   c. see a program about animals   _____

   d. watch a funny film   _____

   e. hear singing   _____

   f. watch a science fiction program _____

   g. see a love story   _____

   h. learn what's happening in the world _____ or _____

   i. be scared   _____ or _____

3. What about you? Look at the TV schedule in Exercise 1. What would you like to watch? Why? Try to use the words *serious, funny, sad, boring,* and *interesting.*

   Example: *I'd like to watch Science Watch. It sounds interesting.*

   _____

4. Write the type of entertainment. Use the words in the box.

> children's program   concert   ~~quiz show~~   shopping program
> science fiction story   soap opera   tragedy   western

And the score is: Alicia 25 and Todd 12.

a. _____quiz show_____

You can buy this wonderful tool for only $29.99 plus shipping.

b. _____

Get off your horses, cowboys.

c. _____

Good-bye boys and girls. See you tomorrow!

d. _____

Look! He's purple! And he has three arms and two heads!

e. _____

I love you. I'll never leave you. I want to marry you and be with you. Always.

f. _____

Romeo and Juliet are dead!

g. _____

Next we will hear Beethoven's Piano Sonata Number 3.

h. _____

5. What about you? What is your favourite TV program? Complete the information.

Name of program: _____

Type of program: _____

Day: _____

Time: _____

Channel: _____

Other information: _____

_____

_____

_____

Challenge Look at **page 185** in this book. Follow the instructions.

Holidays

1. Look in your dictionary. Write the holiday next to the date.

   a. July 1   <u>Canada Day</u>   **d.** Jan. 1   _____

   b. Feb. 14 _____   **e.** Dec. 25   _____

   c. Oct. 31 _____   **f.** 2nd Mon. in Oct. _____

2. Write the names of the holidays on the cards. Then circle the correct words to complete the descriptions.

a. The card is for <u>Canada Day /</u> <u>New Year's Day.</u>

b. There's a <u>feast / jack-o'-lantern</u> on the card.

c. There's a <u>jack-o'-lantern / turkey</u>. It's part of a <u>costume / feast</u>.

d. There's a red <u>heart / mask</u>.

e. There's a <u>flag / tree</u> with <u>hearts / ornaments</u>.

_____ **Challenge** Make a holiday card.

A Party

1. Look in your dictionary. Who's...? Check (✓) the correct columns.

	TOM	SUE	THE GUESTS
a. planning a party	✓		
b. hiding			
c. blowing out candles			
d. answering the door			
e. decorating the house			
f. shouting "surprise!"			
g. lighting the candles			
h. singing "Happy Birthday"			
i. making a wish			
j. opening presents			

2. Melissa is planning a party. Look at her list and the picture. Cross out the things she has already done.

FOR THE PARTY
1. ~~invite guests~~
2. buy gift
3. buy card
4. wrap gift
5. decorate house
6. bake cake
7. buy candles

3. What about you? Describe a party you went to.

Type of party: _____   Place: _____

Time: _____   Number of guests: _____

Check (✓) the things that happened. Did people...?

☐ decorate the room   ☐ shout "surprise!"   ☐ sing "Happy Birthday"
☐ light candles   ☐ open presents   ☐ Other: _____

Challenge Plan a party. Make a list of things you will do before the party and at the party.

▶ **Go to page 181 for Another Look (Unit 12).**

Another Look (Unit 1)

"C" Search

Look at the picture. There are more than 15 items that begin with the letter **c.** Find and circle them.

Make a list of the items that you circled. Use your own paper.

Example: *coins*

Picture Crossword Puzzle

Complete the puzzle.

Picture Word Search

Find and circle the 15 house words. The words go → and ↓.

```
H  U  G  M  A  I  L  B  O  X
I  R  A  A  N  C  O  O  L  R
M  I  R  R  O  R  C  W  D  B
B  L  A  K  R  I  K  S  M  U
L  I  G  H  T  B  U  L  B  S
E  L  E  V  O  T  E  E  O  H
N  I  N  W  I  N  D  O  W  I
D  D  O  L  L  S  H  E  L  F
E  I  W  H  E  I  A  L  O  W
R  A  K  E  T  M  O  U  S  E
```

"C" Search

Look at the picture. There are more than 25 items that begin with the letter **c.**
Find and circle them.

Make a list of the items that you circled. Use your own paper.

Example: *coconut*

Another Look (Unit 5)

Picture Word Search

Find and circle the 16 clothes words. The words go → and ↓.

```
S  W  E  A  T  S  H  I  R  T
O  A  T  S  E  O  A  B  I  U
C  L  A  V  E  S  T  E  N  R
K  L  E  O  T  A  R  D  G  T
S  E  T  E  N  N  O  R  O  L
S  T  H  R  E  A  D  O  B  E
B  R  A  O  E  M  I  R  O  N
E  L  M  E  D  I  U  M  O  E
L  O  C  A  L  R  P  A  T  C
T  E  N  J  E  A  N  S  S  K
```

SIZE
M

Picture Crossword Puzzle

Complete the puzzle.

¹T	A	²B	L	E	³T		⁴		
					⁵			⁶	
⁷									
⁸		⁹		¹⁰					
						¹¹			
		¹²		¹³					
¹⁴					¹⁵		¹⁶		
	¹⁷								

ACROSS ➡

DOWN ⬇

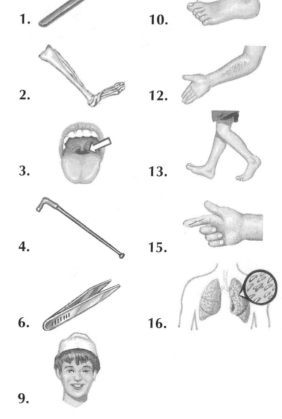

1.

5.

7.

8.

11.

14.

15.

17.

1.

2.

3.

4.

6.

9.

10.

12.

13.

15.

16.

175

Another Look (Unit 7)

"C" Search

Look at the picture. There are more than 12 items that begin with the letter **c.**
Find and circle them.

Make a list of the items that you circled. Use your own paper.

Example: *coffee shop*

Where have all the flowers gone?

Look at the picture. Circle all the flowers.

Write the location of the flowers. Use your own paper.

Example: *On the bus*

Scrambled Notes

Unscramble the words for these areas of study.

English Composition
gEnshil poCmsooniti

rapagrhap _____

nestneec ___paragraph___

locno _____

deti _____

---

thaM

aqsure _____

buce _____

midateer _____

lagerab _____

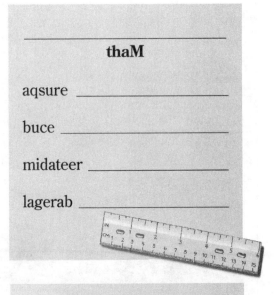

---

cisMu

lufet _____

onipa _____

putrmet _____

cacrodnia _____

---

greyohGap

aslind _____

eacon _____

verir _____

palsin _____

---

cicSeen

eldis _____

mota _____

msirp _____

mechisytr _____

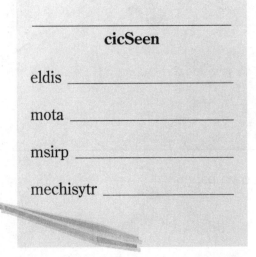

---

heT vsUnieer

letecopse _____

rurMyec _____

lagyax _____

nocteslltanio _____

Picture Crossword Puzzle

Complete the puzzle.

ACROSS

DOWN

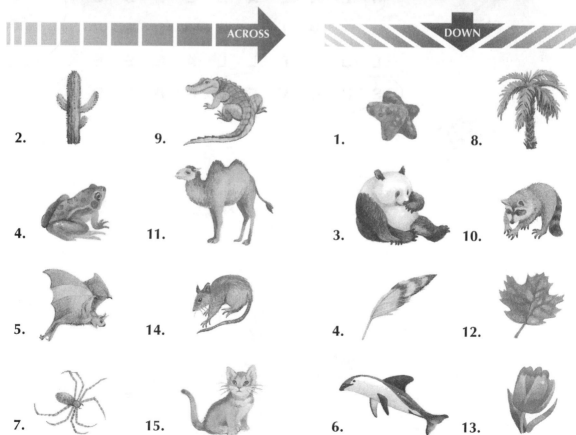

2.

9.

4.

11.

5.

14.

7.

15.

1.

3.

4.

6.

8.

10.

12.

13.

Picture Word Search

Find and circle the 16 work words. The words go → and ↓.

```
C  L  I  P  B  O  A  R  D     E
A  E  N  A  P  O  I  S  O  N
S  T  A  P  L  E  R  T  C  M
H  O  P  E  I  R  N  U  T  O
I  B  A  R  N  A  R  W  O  U
E  O  X  C  P  L  I  E  R  S
R  L  E  L  A  B  E  L  D  E
A  T  M  I  L  A  D  D  E  R
L  O  O  P  L  L  A  E  S  E
S  H  O  V  E  L  N  R  K  D
```

"C" Search

Look at the picture. There are more than 20 items and activities that begin with the letter **c**. Find and circle them.

Make a list of the items and activities that you circled. Use your own paper.

Example: *cooler*

Challenge for page 8

Lu is talking to her friend, Ana. Complete the conversation.

_____, Ana.

Hi!

_____

Thanks!

_____

Bye.

Lu greets Ana.   **Lu compliments Ana.**   **They end the conversation.**

Challenge for page 20

Which coins or bills do you need for a...?

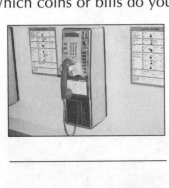

a. _____

b. _____

c. _____

d. _____

e. _____

f. _____

Challenge for page 21

Complete the sales slip for the item.

```
Cheap Eddie's          6/11/02

    Every Day Is a Sale Day!

1 _____    _____
tax @ 7%                 _____
Total                    _____
Amount tendered      $30.00
Change                   _____

        Thank You
```

Challenge for pages 28–29

Complete the timeline for yourself or someone you know.

Challenge for pages 30–31

What do you do when you feel…?

a. nervous   **b.** bored   **c.** homesick   **d.** confused   **e.** angry

Example: *When I feel nervous, I go for a walk.*

Challenge for page 57

Fill in the blanks.

a. _____ 237 mL _____ = _____ 1 cup _____

b. _____ 15 mL _____ = _____

c. _____ 5 mL _____ = _____

d. _____ 1000 g _____ = _____

Challenge for page 85

Look at page 85 in this book. What does the doctor do? What does the dentist do? What do both the doctor and dentist do? Put the words from Exercise 2 in the correct space.

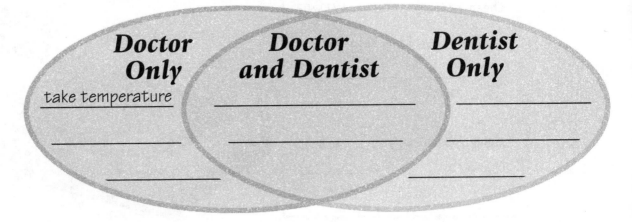

Doctor Only

take temperature

_____

_____

Doctor and Dentist

_____

_____

Dentist Only

_____

_____

_____

Challenge for page 104

1. Survey your classmates. Which forms of transportation do they use? Complete the chart.

FORM OF TRANSPORTATION	NUMBER OF STUDENTS

2. Make a bar graph. Use the information from your chart in Exercise 1.

Challenge for page 114

Write the name(s) of…

a. the Prime Minister of Canada   _____

b. the Governor General   _____

c. your Lieutenant Governor (or Commissioner)   _____

d. your Member of Parliament (MP)   _____

e. the elected representative to your provincial or territorial government   _____

f. your mayor or reeve   _____

Challenge for pages 124–125

Complete the information for a classmate.

_____'S COUNTRY	CONTINENT	NUMBER OF NEIGHBOURS	POPULATION
_____	_____	_____	_____

Write the names of the country's neighbours.

_____

Challenge for pages 142–143

What can you use these office supplies for? Which do you prefer? Why?

a. appointment book / desk calendar   _____

b. typewriter / computer   _____

c. telephone / fax   _____

d. staples / paper clips   _____

e. clear tape / packing tape   _____

f. address book / rotary card file   _____

g. file folders / big envelopes   _____

Challenge for pages 162–163

Find out about some other games. Complete the chart.

NAME OF THE GAME	TYPE OF GAME (BOARD/CARD/VIDEO)	COUNTRY PEOPLE PLAY THE GAME IN	NUMBER OF PLAYERS

Challenge for pages 166–167

Look in the newspaper or ask classmates for the name of a....

sitcom   _____

game show   _____

sad movie   _____

serious TV program   _____

soap opera   _____

radio program   _____

talk show   _____

ANSWER KEY

UNIT 1

Pages 2 and 3 A Classroom

Exercise 1
a. 1   b. 1   c. 13   d. 2   e. 1   f. 1

Exercise 2
Items checked:
pencil sharpener   spiral notebook
pencils   notebook paper
ruler

Exercise 3
2. overhead progector → overhead projector
3. computter → computer
5. chawk → chalk
7. alfabet → alphabet
10. bulletin bord → bulletin board

Exercise 4
a. 8   b. 1   c. 2   d. 9   e. 10   f. 7
g. 5   h. 6   i. 3   j. 4

Page 4 Personal Information

Exercise 1
a. V6B 5G3   b. 604   c. 10   d. 476 012 000

Exercise 2
a. 6   b. 8   c. 5   d. 1   e. 3   f. 4
g. 9   h. 7   i. 2

Page 5 School

Exercise 1
People:
teacher   counsellor
principal   administrative assistant

Places:
classroom   washrooms
auditorium   gym
cafeteria   track
lunch benches   field
library   principal's office
bleachers   counsellor's office
lockers   main office

Exercise 2
Auditorium C   Library G
Cafeteria D   Lockers J
Classrooms A, B, H, I   Men's Washrooms F
Gym K   Women's Washrooms E

Pages 6 and 7 Studying

Exercise 1
a. False b. True c. False d. True e. False

Exercise 2
a. 3   b. 2   c. 4   d. 8   e. 6   f. 7
g. 9   h. 5   i. 1

Exercise 3
1. a. in   b. up   c. out
2. a. match   b. spell   c. talk
3. *Words underlined:* say, share, spell
   Words circled: copy, circle, check
4. check   circle   copy   help   read   say
   share   spell
5. a. 3   b. 1   c. 2

Challenge
a. thimble   b. page 73   c.

Page 8 Everyday Conversation

Exercise 1
a. 5   b. 2   c. 4   d. 3   e. 1

Exercise 2
a. Ming, this is Kim.   b. Did you say *Kim*?
c. How are things?   d. That's a great jacket.
e. Thank you.   f. See you.

Challenge (page 182)
Possible conversations include:
Lu: Hi/Hello/Good morning, Ana.
Ana: Hi!
Lu: That's a nice/pretty sweater/scarf/hat.
Ana: Thanks.
Lu: Bye/Goodbye/See you.
Ana: Bye.

Page 9 The Telephone

Exercise 1
a. 4   b. 1   c. 5   d. 3   e. 6   f. 2

Exercise 2
a. 2   b. 1   c. 5   d. 4   e. 6   f. 3
Filled-in blank: pay

Exercise 3
a. phone   b. answering machine
c. cellular phone   d. pager   e. cordless phone

Page 10 Weather

Exercise 1
warm   freezing   hot

Exercise 2
True statements: b, c, f, h, i

Page 11 Describing Things

Exercise 1
a. little   d. expensive
b. thin   e. beautiful
c. light   f. fast

Exercise 2

a. False. The classroom is quiet.
b. True.
c. True.
d. False. The teacher's desk is neat.
e. False. The bookcase is messy.
f. True.
g. False. The chairs are hard.

Page 12 Colours

Exercise 1

a. green
b. purple
c. blue
d. orange

Exercise 2

Women's favourite colours:

1. blue
2. red
3. pink
4. green
5. purple
6. yellow
7. black
8. white
9. brown and grey

Men's favourite colours:

1. blue
2. red
3. green
4. brown
5. black
6. grey
7. purple
8. pink, white, and yellow

Page 13 Prepositions

Exercise 1

a. True b. False c. True d. False e. True

Exercise 2

a. on b. below c. next d. above e. between
f. under g. beside h. left i. in

Pages 14 and 15
Numbers and Measurement

Exercise 1

a. cardinal
b. fraction
c. Roman
d. ordinal
e. per cent
f. cardinal

Exercise 2

Word	Number	Roman Numeral
ten	10	X
three	3	III
fifteen	15	XV
fifty	50	L
twenty	20	XX
one hundred	100	C
five hundred	500	D
one thousand	1000	M

Exercise 3

a. first
b. fourth
c. fifth
d. second
e. sixth
f. third

Exercise 4

Spanish: 50%
French: 5%
Japanese: 10%
Russian: 10%
Chinese: 25%

a. fifty per cent
b. twenty-five per cent
c. five per cent
d. ten per cent
e. ten per cent

Exercise 5

a. One-fourth
b. One-third
c. One-fourth
d. One-half

Pages 16 and 17 Time

Exercise 1

a. half past ten
b. a quarter to three
c. three-fifteen
d. six-twenty

Exercise 2

a. 3   b. 7   c. 6   d. 2   e. 1   f. 4
g. 8   h. 5

Exercise 3

| 4:10 | 6:30 | 8:00 | 11:45 |

Exercise 5

a. Atlantic
b. Central
c. Mountain
d. Pacific

Exercise 6

a. 7:00 in the evening
b. 5:00 in the afternoon
c. 10:30 at night
d. 12:00 noon
e. 1:00 in the afternoon
f. 2:00 in the morning
g. 8:00 at night/8:00 in the evening
h. 12:00 midnight
i. 11:00 in the morning
j. 6:00 in the evening
k. 9:00 in the morning
l. 1:00 in the morning

Challenge

Eastern time: Montréal, Havana, New York City, Panama
Central time: Houston, Mexico City
Atlantic time: Halifax, San Juan
Pacific time: Los Angeles

Pages 18 and 19 The Calendar

Exercise 1
a. 31   b. 5   c. 4   d. 23   e. 4   f. 3

Exercise 2
a. False   b. False   c. True   d. True   e. False
f. True   g. False   h. True   i. False   j. True

Exercise 4
Winter: January, February
Spring: April, May
Summer: July, August
Fall: October, November

Exercise 5
1. c   2. d   3. a   4. f   5. e   6. b

Page 20 Money

Exercise 1
a. $3.41   b. $185.00   c. $188.41

Exercise 2
a. $5.10   b. $.50 or 50¢
c. $.25 or 25¢   d. $160.00
e. $5.28   f. $46.00

Exercise 3
(The date and student's signature will vary.)
Pay to the order of: Mary Johnson
Amount: $25.00
Amount in words: Twenty-five and ⁰⁰/ₓₓ
Form of payment checked: personal cheque

Page 21 Shopping

Exercise 1
a. three   d. is   g. green
b. sale price   e. gives
c. total   f. keeps

Exercise 2
a. receipt   d. pay   g. return
b. price   e. change   h. Keep
c. sales   f. exchange

Challenge (page 183)

1 cassette player	25.00
tax @ 7%	1.75
Total	26.75
Amount tendered	$30.00
Change	3.25

UNIT 2

Page 22 Age and Physical Description

Exercise 1
a. 9   b. 4   c. 2   d. 3

Exercise 2
Words circled:
Tall   cute
Attractive   30-year-old
middle-aged   short
average weight   18-year-old
Attractive   average weight
slim   young
elderly   physically challenged
Short   heavyset

1. c   2. e   3. a   4. d   5. f   6. b

Page 23 Describing Hair

Exercise 1
a. 2   b. 7*   c. 2   d. 1**   e. 3   f. 2
*9 *if you include the two in the mirror reflection*
**2 *if you include the one in the mirror reflection*

Exercise 2
Items checked: cut, colour
a. short   b. straight   c. brown   d. part

Pages 24 and 25 Family

Exercise 1

Male	*Female*	*Male or Female*
brother	niece	cousin
husband	daughter	parent
son	grandmother	
uncle		

Exercise 2
a. False   b. True   c. False   d. True   e. True
f. False   g. True   h. True   i. True   j. False

Exercise 4
a. former wife   d. brother
b. mother   e. stepsister
c. father   f. stepfather

Exercise 5
1. She's married.   4. She's a single mother.
2. She has a baby.   5. She's remarried.
3. She's divorced.   6. She's a stepmother.

Exercise 6
a. mother   d. son
b. father   e. stepbrother
c. stepfather

Pages 26 and 27 Daily Routines

Exercise 1
6:00 wake up
6:30 get dressed
7:00 eat breakfast
7:30 take the children to school
8:00 drive to work
5:00 leave work
5:30 pick up the children
6:30 have dinner
8:00 relax
8:30 exercise
11:00 go to sleep

Exercise 2
1. d   2. e   3. b   4. c   5. a   6. f
7. g

Exercise 3
a. relaxes   f. makes   k. makes
b. gets up   g. leaves   l. takes
c. takes   h. goes   m. eats
d. eats   i. picks up   n. watches
e. drives   j. gets   o. goes

Pages 28 and 29 Life Events

Exercise 1
1925 was born   1956 went to college
1930 started school   1958 got married
1940 immigrated   1960 had a baby
1942 graduated   1971 bought a house
1944 joined the army   1985 became a grandfather
1949 became a citizen 1997 died

Exercise 2
a. was   e. got   i. had
b. graduated f. rented   j. died
c. learned   g. fell
d. moved   h. got

Exercise 3
a. 4   b. 3   c. 1   d. 5   e. 2

Pages 30 and 31 Feelings

Exercise 1
Words that end in -y:
thirsty   hungry   angry
sleepy   lonely   happy

Words that end in -ed:
disgusted   scared   frustrated
worried   embarrassed surprised
relieved   bored   tired
excited   confused

Exercise 2
a. relieved   e. happy   i. disgusted
b. scared   f. sleepy/tired   j. confused
c. angry   g. hungry
d. surprised   h. thirsty

Exercise 3
☺

calm	full	proud
comfortable	in love	well

☹

bored	in pain	uncomfortable
homesick	nervous	sick

Exercise 4
a. comfortable   d. proud
b. in love   e. sick/in pain
c. homesick   f. nervous

Pages 32 and 33 A Graduation

Exercise 1
a. False   b. True   c. True   d. False

Exercise 2
1. e   2. f   3. d   4. a   5. c   6. h
7. g   8. b

Exercise 3
b

Exercise 4
a. party   c. gifts   e. caterer
b. hugging   d. guest   f. buffet

UNIT 3

Page 34 Places to Live

Exercise 1
a. university residence   b. nursing home
c. shelter

Exercise 2
a. city   d. 35%
b. country   e. city
c. houses

Page 35 Finding a Home

Exercise 1
a. rent   d. house
b. manager   e. man and woman make
c. $450   f. mortgage

Exercise 2

	Rent an apartment	Buy a house
a.	✔	
b.		✔
c.	✔	
d.		✔
e.		✔
f.	✔	✔
g.	✔	
h.		✔
i.	✔	✔
j.	✔	✔

Pages 36 and 37 Apartments

Exercise 1
a. doorman   d. manager/superintendent
b. tenant   e. neighbour/tenant
c. landlord

Exercise 2
a. False   b. False   c. True   d. False   e. True
f. False

Exercise 3
a. fire exit, elevator   c. garbage chute
b. mailbox   d. intercom

Page 38 A House

Exercise 1
a. Closed   c. Open   e. Open
b. Open   d. Closed   f. Closed

Exercise 2
a. False   b. True   c. True   d. False   e. False
f. True   g. False

Challenge
a. This is a one-storey house.
d. There is a chair on the deck.
e. The TV antenna is on the roof.
g. The fence is in the front yard.

Page 39 A Yard

Exercise 1
a. on the patio   d. on the patio
b. on the lawn   e. on the lawn
c. on the lawn   f. on the patio

Exercise 2
Garden tools:	Vegetation:	Containers:
pruning shears	bush	flowerpot
rake	flower	garbage can
shovel	hedge	watering can
trowel	lawn	wheelbarrow

Exercise 3
Items checked:
water the plants
trim the hedge
plant trees

Page 40 A Kitchen

Exercise 1
a. under the cabinet   d. on the stove/burner
b. on the counter   e. under the oven
c. on the cutting board   f. under the sink

Exercise 2
Things that last 10 years:
blender   dishwasher
coffee maker   pan
toaster   electric can opener

Things that last 15 years:
stove   refrigerator

Page 41 A Dining Area

Exercise 1
a. True   b. True   c. False   d. False   e. False
f. True   g. False

Exercise 2
a. bowl   e. napkin
b. plate   f. spoons
c. placemat   g. knife
d. forks   h. glass

Page 42 A Living Room

Exercise 1
a. 3   b. 6   c. 1   d. 1   e. 3

Exercise 2
Items crossed out:
couch   track lighting
stereo   plant
wall unit   magazine holder
bookcase   logs

Page 43 A Bathroom

Exercise 1

	Sink	Bathtub/Shower	Wall	Floor
a.		✔	✔	
b.	✔	✔		
c.	✔	✔		
d.		✔	✔	✔
e.		✔		✔
f.	✔	✔		
g.	✔			

Exercise 2
a. bath mat   e. toilet brush
b. wastebasket   f. washcloth
c. hand towel   g. scale
d. soap dish

Page 44   A Bedroom

Exercise 1
a. purple   b. blue   c. pink and white

Exercise 2
a. mirror   d. lampshade
b. headboard   e. dresser
c. lamp   f. photographs

Exercise 3
a. clock radio   d. curtains
b. blanket   e. closet
c. mattress

Page 45   A Children's Bedroom

Exercise 1
a. night light   c. baby monitor
b. bumper pad   d. smoke detector

Exercise 2
Possible answers include:
under the bunk bed
under the comforter/in the bunk bed
in the crib
on the chest of drawers
on the change table
on the diaper pail
on the blocks
under the colouring book
on the ball
in the cradle
in the toy chest
in the dollhouse

Page 46   Housework

Exercise 1
a. recycling the newspapers
b. putting away the toys
c. making the bed
d. drying the dishes

Exercise 2
Items checked:
wash the sheets
dust the dresser
clean the sink

Page 47   Cleaning Supplies

Exercise 1
Possible answers include:

Windows:
glass cleaner   sponge
squeegee   stepladder
rubber gloves   rags

Floor:
broom   dust mop
dust pan   scrub brush
vacuum cleaner   bucket/pail
vacuum cleaner attachments   sponge
vacuum cleaner bag   rags
wet mop

Dishes:
rubber gloves   dish towel
steel-wool soap pads   sponge
dishwashing liquid

Exercise 2
1. d   2. h   3. g   4. c   5. e   6. a
7. b   8. f   9. i

Pages 48 and 49
Household Problems and Repairs

Exercise 1
a. roofer   e. locksmith
b. exterminator   f. carpenter
c. electrician   g. repair person
d. plumber

Exercise 2
a. False. The bathtub tap is dripping.
b. True
c. False. There are cockroaches near the sink.
d. True
e. False. The toilet is overflowing.
f. False. The wall is cracked.

Exercise 3

1. exterminator 555-4789
   a. cockroaches

2. plumber   555-2233
   a. dripping tap
   b. overflowing toilet
   c. stopped up sink

3. electrician   555-2656
   a. broken light/the light isn't working

4. repair person 555-8356
   a. broken window
   b. cracked wall

UNIT 4

Page 50 Fruit

Exercise 1
a. peaches   d. cherries, strawberries
b. plums   e. papayas
c. avocados   f. bananas

Exercise 2
First row across:

pineapples   avocados   pears

Second row across:

oranges   grapefruit   limes *or* lemons/
                             lemons *or* limes

Third row across:

strawberries   apples   grapes

Page 51 Vegetables

Exercise 1
Yellow/Orange: **Red:**
carrots   radishes
squash   tomatoes
yams   beets
corn   chili peppers
onions

Green:
lettuce   cucumbers
cabbage   broccoli
zucchini   scallions
green peppers   peas
celery   artichokes
parsley   asparagus
spinach   green beans

Exercise 2
a. spinach   c. beets   e. tomatoes
b. broccoli   d. carrots   f. lettuce

Page 52 Meat and Poultry

Exercise 1
With bones:
steak   lamb shanks
beef ribs   leg of lamb
ham   lamb chops
pork chops

Boneless:
beef roast   liver
stewing beef   tripe
ground beef   bacon
veal cutlets   sausage

Exercise 2
a. 3–4 hours
b. 3 hours (180 minutes)
c. 6 minutes (3 minutes each side)
d. 3 hours (180 minutes)
e. 20 minutes (10 minutes each side)
f. 1 1/4 hours (1 hour 15 minutes)

Exercise 3
a. breast   b. wing   c. drumstick   d. thigh

Page 53 Deli and Seafood

Exercise 1
a. halibut   e. filet of sole   i. scallops
b. catfish   f. mussels   j. lobster
c. salmon steak g. crab   k. shrimp
d. trout   h. clams   l. oysters

Exercise 2
Items checked:
Meat: smoked turkey, salami
Bread: rye
Cheese: Swiss
Sides: potato salad, coleslaw

Pages 54 and 55 The Supermarket

Exercise 1
a. canned goods   aisle 1B
b. meat and poultry   aisle 1A
c. produce   across from the dairy section
d. baked goods   aisle 2B
e. dairy   behind the produce section
f. beverages   to the left of the doors
g. frozen foods   to the right of the produce
                       section
h. baking products   aisle 5B
i. paper products   aisle 6B
j. snack foods   near the checkout

Exercise 2
a. Manager   e. cashier
b. bottle return   f. Bagger
c. cart   g. plastic
d. checkouts

Exercise 3
Canned goods: tuna, beans
Frozen foods: ice cream
Baking products: flour, sugar, oil
Dairy section: eggs, yogurt, butter, milk,
 cheddar cheese
Beverages: bottled water, pop
Paper products: aluminum foil, plastic wrap
Baked goods: bread, lemon cake, rolls
Snack foods: potato chips, gum

Exercise 4
Items crossed off list:

tuna	potato chips	pop
eggs	butter	cheese
bread	milk	
ice cream	oil	

Page 56
Containers and Packaged Foods

Exercise 1
a. can   b. box   c. jar   d. container

Exercise 2
a. tube   b. carton   c. six-pack   d. bottle
e. bag   f. loaf   g. package   h. roll

Exercise 3
2 tubes of toothpaste   2 bags of potato chips
1 carton of orange juice 1 loaf of bread
1 six-pack of pop   1 package of cookies
2 bottles of water   3 rolls of paper towels

Page 57   Weights and Measures

Exercise 1
a. 2   b. 3   c. 7   d. 4   e. 5   f. 1
g. 6

Exercise 2
a. 1.5 kilograms of potatoes
b. 1 litre of apple juice
c. 750 millilitres of flour
d. 2 litres of milk
e. 3 tablespoons or 45 millilitres of butter/margarine
f. 3 teaspoons or 15 millilitres of sugar

Challenge (page 183)
a. 237 mL = 1 cup
b. 15 mL = 1 tbsp.
c. 5 mL = 1 tsp.
d. 1000 g = 1 kg

Page 58   Food Preparation

Exercise 1
Words underlined:

Chop	Add	Pour
Peel	cook	Bake
grate	Stir	
Grease	Add	

Exercise 2
a. 2   b. 7   c. 1   d. 3   e. 4   f. 8
g. 5   h. 6

Exercise 3
Words circled:
a. Boil   d. Fry
b. Slice   e. Mix
c. Chop   f. Sauté

Page 59   Kitchen Utensils

Exercise 1
a. False   b. True   c. True   d. False   e. True
f. False

Exercise 2
a. 6   b. 7   c. 1   d. 8   e. 3   f. 5
g. 9   h. 4   i. 2

Exercise 3
a. can opener   d. egg beater   g. cookie sheet
b. garlic press   e. mixing bowl   h. double boiler
c. rolling pin   f. cake pan   i. pot holder

Page 60   Fast Food

Exercise 1
A straw:

pop	iced tea	milkshake

Your fingers:

hamburger	taco
french fries	nachos
cheeseburger	frozen yogurt
hot dog	muffin
pizza	doughnut

Exercise 2
Items checked: cheese, lettuce, ketchup, relish

Exercise 3
1. mayonnaise   3. ketchup
2. sugar   4. mustard/relish

Page 61   A Coffee Shop Menu

Exercise 1
a. sausage, toast   e. baked potato
b. grilled cheese sandwich   f. garlic bread
c. Fried fish, rice pilaf   g. pie
d. Pancakes

Exercise 2

roast chicken	tea
mashed potatoes	waffles (and syrup)
chef's salad	coffee/decaf coffee
(pineapple) cake	

Pages 62 and 63 A Restaurant

Exercise 1
a. dishwasher
b. patron/diner
c. server/waiter/waitress

d. chef
e. server/waitress/waiter
f. hostess

Exercise 2
Items checked:

salad plate
bread-and-butter plate
wine glass
cup
saucer

salad fork
steak knife
teaspoon
soup spoon

Exercise 3

black bean soup	3.50
house salad	2.50
grilled salmon	15.50
peas	1.50
french fries	1.50
cherry pie w. vanilla ice cream	4.00
coffee	1.50
Subtotal	30.00
Tax (7%)	2.10
Total	32.10

Exercise 4
a. $30.00   b. $4.50   c. table

UNIT 5

Pages 64 and 65 Clothing I

Exercise 1
a. orange
b. blue
c. (light) brown

d. green
e. grey
f. purple

Exercise 2
Women:

blouse
dress
evening gown
jumper

leggings
maternity dress
skirt
tunic

Both Women and Men:

jeans
pants
suit
sweater

T-shirt
turtleneck
uniform
vest

Men:

sports coat
sports shirt

three-piece suit
tuxedo

Exercise 3
a. blue jeans and white T-shirt
b. evening gown
c. dress
d. suit
e. sweatpants and sweatshirt

Exercise 4
1. e   2. d   3. a   4. c   5. b

Page 66 Clothing II

Exercise 1
a. True   b. True   c. False   d. False

Exercise 2
a. parka
b. toque
c. mittens
d. jacket
e. earmuffs
f. scarf

g. straw hat
h. swimsuit
i. cover-up
j. umbrella
k. sunglasses

Page 67 Clothing III

Exercise 1
a. black
b. blue
c. black
d. grey

e. green
f. (light) blue
g. red
h. (dark) blue

Exercise 2

2 bras	24.00
1 half slip	8.50
1 camisole	15.00
3 pr briefs/underpants	15.00
2 pr pantyhose	9.00
8 pr socks	16.00
Total	87.50

Pages 68 and 69 Shoes and Accessories

Exercise 1
a. 2   b. 3   c. 8   d. 8   e. 2   f. 10*
*8 on rack, 1 on customer, 1 on salesclerk

Exercise 2
backpacks
belts
bracelets
chains
earrings
handkerchiefs
hats
key chains

necklaces
pins
purses
rings
scarves
ties
wallets
watches

a. 7   b. 9   c. 1   d. 8   e. 9   f. 3
g. 3   h. 5   i. 1   j. 2   k. 4   l. 10
m. 6   n. 7   o. 4   p. 2

Exercise 3
a. belt
b. bracelet
c. wallet
d. suspenders
e. pin

Exercise 4
a. boots
b. loafers
c. oxfords
d. hiking boots
e. running shoes
f. track shoes
g. sandals
h. high heels

Pages 70 and 71 Describing Clothes

Exercise 1
a. True b. True c. False d. True e. False
f. False

Exercise 2
a. 4 b. 8 c. 6 d. 1 e. 7 f. 3
g. 2 h. 5

Exercise 3
a. too short
b. too high/too narrow/too tight
c. too wide/too loose
d. too light
e. too casual

Exercise 4
a. small
b. large
c. synthetic
d. solid
e. light
f. baggy

Page 72 Doing the Laundry

Exercise 1
a. on the shelf
b. on the dryer
c. on the ironing board
d. on the clothesline

Exercise 2
a. 5 b. 3 c. 2 d. 7 e. 1 f. 6
g. 4

Page 73 Sewing and Alterations

Exercise 1
a. customer b. tailor c. dressmaker

Exercise 2
Items checked:
sew on buttons   take in waistband
shorten hemline   repair pocket

Exercise 3
1 tape measure   1 (pair of) scissors
1 pin cushion   1 thimble
4 pins   3 buttons
3 needles   2 spools of thread
2 safety pins

UNIT 6

Pages 74 and 75 The Body

Exercise 1
a. neck
b. abdomen
c. knee
d. brain
e. toenail
f. ear

Exercise 2
a. hair
b. forehead
c. ear
d. eyebrow
e. eyelashes
f. eyelid
g. eye
h. cheek
i. nose
j. lip
k. gums
l. teeth
m. mouth
n. jaw
o. chin

Exercise 3
Items checked:
arms   knees
calves   legs*
elbows   neck
fingers   shoulders
most of legs are not covered

Exercise 4
a. 4 b. 9 c. 3 d. 5 e. 6 f. 11
g. 2 h. 7 i. 10 j. 1 k. 8

Pages 76 and 77 Personal Hygiene

Exercise 1
a. hair spray
b. sunscreen
c. hair clip
d. eyebrow pencil
e. deodorant
f. moisturizer
g. comb

Exercise 2
1. d 2. a 3. e 4. c 5. b 6. f
7. g

Exercise 3
Items checked:
blow dryer   deodorant
brush   lipstick
cologne/perfume   nail clipper
comb   shaving cream
curling iron   sunscreen
dental floss   talcum powder

Exercise 4
Items checked in chart of Exercise 3:
conditioner   shower cap   toothpaste
shampoo   soap

Exercise 5
bobby pins   mouthwash   toothbrush
emery board   nail polish
mascara   razor

Page 78 Symptoms and Injuries

Exercise 1
a. True   b. True   c. False   d. True   e. False
f. True   g. False

Exercise 2
Items checked:
toothaches   nasal congestion
stomachaches   rashes
sore throats   cough

Page 79
Illnesses and Medical Conditions

Exercise 1
a. lungs   d. lungs
b. heart   e. intestines
c. pancreas   f. blood

Exercise 2
Items checked:
chicken pox   mumps
allergies   ear infections

Pages 80 and 81 Health Care

Exercise 1
a. pharmacist   d. audiologist
b. physiotherapist   e. orthopedist
c. optometrist

Exercise 2
a. False   b. False   c. False   d. True   e. False
f. True   g. False

Exercise 3
a. 4   c. 1   e. 3
b. 5   d. 2

Exercise 4
a. pharmacy   e. eat cheese
b. prescription medication   f. dosage
c. capsules   g. March 2001
d. warning label

Page 82 Medical Emergencies

Exercise 1
a. True   b. True   c. False   d. False   e. True
f. False

Exercise 2
a. fell   e. swallowed poison
b. bled   f. got a shock
c. broke bones   g. got frostbite
d. got blisters

Page 83 First Aid

Exercise 1
a. splint
b. antihistamine cream
c. ice pack or elastic bandage
d. antibacterial ointment or hydrogen peroxide

Exercise 2
Items checked:
adhesive bandage   ice pack
antibacterial ointment   sterile pad
gauze   tweezers
hydrogen peroxide

Page 84 Clinics

Exercise 1
a. nurse   d. patient
b. receptionist   e. dentist
c. orthodontist   f. dental hygienist

Exercise 2
a. 6   b. 5   c. 1   d. 3   e. 2   f. 4

Page 85 Medical and Dental Exams

Exercise 1
a. True   b. True   c. False   d. False   e. True

Exercise 2
a. take temperature   e. take an X-ray
b. clean teeth   f. give a shot
c. pull a tooth   g. fill a cavity
d. draw blood   h. examine eyes

Challenge (page 184)
Doctor: *Dentist:*
take temperature   clean teeth
examine eyes   pull a tooth
draw blood   fill a cavity

Doctor and Dentist:
give a shot   take an X-ray

Pages 86 and 87 A Hospital

Exercise 1
a. bed table   d. bedpan
b. bed control   e. call button
c. hospital gown

Exercise 2
a. 2   b. 5   c. 4   d. 3   e. 9   f. 8
g. 6   h. 1   i. 7

Exercise 3
a. nurse
b. volunteer
c. RN (registered nurse)
d. RNA (registered nursing assistant)
e. paramedic
f. patient
g. surgeon
h. surgical nurse
i. anaesthetist

Exercise 4
a. 3   b. 6   c. 2   d. 1   e. 5   f. 4

UNIT 7

Pages 88 and 89 City Streets

Exercise 1
a. furniture store   e. police station
b. movie theatre   f. motel
c. mosque   g. city hall
d. parking garage   h. bakery

Exercise 2
a. 2   b. 12   c. 7   d. 3   e. 8   f. 9
g. 5   h. 10   i. 11   j. 1   k. 4   l. 6

Exercise 3
1. Third and King   5. First and Laurier
2. Fourth and Queen   6. Third and Laurier
3. Second and Mackenzie   7. First and Queen
4. Second and Mackenzie

Pages 90 and 91 An Intersection

Exercise 1
a. True   b. False   c. True   d. False   e. True
f. True   g. True   h. False   i. True   j. False
k. True   l. True

Exercise 2
a. 7   b. 10   c. 6   d. 8   e. 2   f. 9
g. 1   h. 5   i. 3   j. 4

Exercise 3
a. corner   e. drive-thru window
b. mailbox   f. fire hydrant
c. bicycle   g. sign
d. parking space

Exercise 4
a. Laundromat
b. public telephone
c. parking meter
d. crosswalk
e. cart/drive-thru window
f. mailbox

Pages 92 and 93 A Mall

Exercise 1
a. card store   f. pet store
b. optician   g. jewellery store
c. shoe store   h. music store
d. toy store   i. florist
e. video store

Exercise 2
Answers may vary.

Cards/Books	Floor	Services	Floor
card store	1	optician	1
bookstore	2	travel agency	1
		florist	1
Department Store	1, 2	hair salon	1
Entertainment/Music		**Shoes/Accessories**	
music store	2	jewellery store	2
video store	2	shoe store	1
Food		**Specialty Stores**	
food court	2	pet store	1
ice cream stand	1	maternity store	1
candy store	2	electronics store	1
		toy store	2

Exercise 3
a. shoe store   e. video store
b. department store   f. hair salon
c. escalator   g. card store
d. music store

Challenge
Possible answers:

The video store is between the candy store and the maternity shop.

The men's washroom is at the food court, across from the women's washroom, and next to the telephone.

The florist is between the maternity shop and the bookstore.
The pet store is near the information booth, next to the optician.

Pages 94 and 95 A Childcare Centre

Exercise 1
a. False   b. True   c. False   d. False   e. True
f. True

Exercise 2
a. 4   b. 3   c. 1   d. 5   e. 2

Exercise 3
a. a high chair
b. a teething ring
c. a diaper pin
d. a change table
e. a cloth diaper

Exercise 5
a. pacifier
b. diaper pail
c. walker
d. disinfectant
e. rocking chair
f. cubby
g. playpen
h. baby backpack
i. diaper pins

Exercise 6

```
C A R R I A G E H
U N A I W I P E S
B T T F A O A O T
B O T T L E C N R
Y Y L R K P I I O
R P L M E L F P L
Y B E U R E I P L
D I A P E R E L E
I B I A C I R E R
```

Challenge
a. A parent is dropping off a little girl.
c. The girl in blue jeans is playing with toys.
d. A childcare worker is changing diapers.

Page 96 Canada Post

Exercise 1
a. True   b. False   c. True   d. False   e. True

Exercise 2
a. white
b. letter
c. mailing address
d. postmark
e. registered mail

Page 97 A Bank

Exercise 1
a. teller
b. cash
c. vault
d. safety-deposit box
e. cheque book

Exercise 2
a. False   b. True   c. False   d. False   e. True
f. False

Exercise 3
a. Transfer
b. Savings
c. Chequing
d. $40

Challenge
a. This is an ATM receipt.
c. She made a withdrawal.
d. She withdrew $100 from her savings account.
f. Her balance is $6,234.00.

Page 98 A Library

Exercise 1
a. online catalogue/card catalogue
b. periodical section
c. atlas/encyclopedia
d. media section
e. checkout desk
f. reference desk

Exercise 2
a. compact disks/CDs
b. magazines, newspapers
c. atlases
d. books
e. encyclopedias
f. audiocassettes, videocassettes
g. records

Page 99 The Legal System

Exercise 1
a. police officer
b. suspect
c. Crown counsel
d. judge
e. twelve
f. convict

Exercise 2
a. jail (7)
b. trial (4)
c. defendant (6)
d. court (3)
e. released (8)
f. verdict (5)
g. suspect (1)
h. lawyer (2)

Exercise 3
a. handcuffs   b. evidence   c. bail

Page 100 Crime

Exercise 1
Words circled:
Drunk driving   mugging
burglary   illegal drugs
Crimes   assault
vandalism   gang violence
Victim*   murder
*in More Vocabulary section of the Dictionary

Exercise 2
a. 28   b. 41   c. 7   d. 5   e. 2   f. 4
g. 9   h. 13

Page 101 Public Safety

Exercise 1
a. True   b. True   c. False   d. False   e. True

Exercise 2
a. 5   b. 4   c. 2   d. 1   e. 3

Pages 102 and 103
Emergencies and Natural Disasters

Exercise 1
a. mudslide   e. car accident
b. tornado   f. lost child
c. drought   g. blizzard
d. flood

Exercise 2
a. airplane crash
b. Saskatchewan
c. forest fire
d. flood
e. Windsor
f. Toronto

Exercise 3
a. 3   b. 4   c. 1   d. 5   e. 2

UNIT 8

Page 104   Public Transportation

Exercise 1
a. 2   b. 3   c. 1   d. 0

Exercise 2
a. ticket   c. track   e. train
b. transfer   d. passenger

Exercise 3
a. train/bus   b. bus/subway   c. train/bus
d. bus   e. ferry   f. bus/subway/taxi

Page 105   Prepositions of Motion

Exercise 1
a. False   b. True   c. False   d. True   e. False
f. True   g. False

Exercise 2
a. corner   c. over   e. down
b. up   d. bridge   f. across

Exercise 3
walking

Page 106   Cars and Trucks

Exercise 1
a. subcompact   c. tow truck
b. RV   d. tractor trailer

Exercise 2
a. 5   b. 4   c. 3   d. 1   e. 2   f. 6

Page 107   Directions and Traffic Signs

Exercise 1
a. True   b. False   c. True   d. False*   e. True
f. False   g. True   h. False   i. False   j. False
k. True
*Can be True if the bus turns left to pick up the
passengers at the bus stop.

Exercise 2

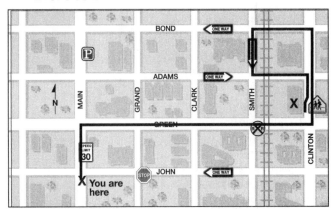

Pages 108 and 109
Parts of a Car and Car Maintenance

Exercise 1
a. turn signal   g. accelerator/gas pedal/
b. windshield wipers   speedometer
c. air conditioning   h. brake pedal
d. jumper cables   i. heater
e. gas gauge   j. speedometer
f. horn/headlights   k. radio
                      l. odometer

Exercise 2
Items checked:
bumper   hubcap
headlight   sideview mirror
hood   windshield

Exercise 3
a. tire (2)   d. temperature gauge (5)
b. oil gauge (1)   e. battery (3)
c. gas gauge (4)

Page 110   An Airport

Exercise 1
a. 2   b. 24   c. 9:00   d. 2

Exercise 2
a. overhead compartment, airplane
b. airsickness bag, airplane
c. carousel, baggage claim area
d. luggage carrier, airline terminal
e. declaration form, customs
f. gate, cockpit

Page 111 A Plane Trip

Exercise 1
Flight number: 508
Destination: St. John's
Departure time: 4:30
Seat number: 14F

Exercise 2
a. finding his seat
b. going through security
c. buying his ticket
d. looking for the emergency exit
e. experiencing turbulence
f. claiming his baggage

Exercise 3
Items checked:
got her boarding pass
boarded the plane
found her seat
looked at the emergency card*
requested a pillow

*if student believes she is putting the card back.

UNIT 9

Page 112 Types of Schools

Exercise 1
a. private school
b. preschool
c. university
d. Catholic school
e. public school
f. vocational school/
   trade school

Exercise 2
a. 2   b. 3   c. 5   d. 1   e. 4   f. 6

Page 113 English Composition

Exercise 1
a. True   b. False   c. False   d. True   e. False
f. False   g. True

Exercise 2
a. 6   b. 7   c. 1   d. 5   e. 8   f. 2
g. 3   h. 4

Exercise 3

Name: Sonia Hernandez

We're moving to San Diego⊙California next
September. (Im) worried. Will I like it? Where
will we live⊙My father says, "Don't worry.⊙"
He says that I'll make new friends. My mother
says that soon San Diego will feel like home.
"But I'm happy here?" I exclaim. I watch my
father's face and listen to my mother's words.
I feel better.

Page 114 Government and Citizenship in Canada

Exercise 1

Canadian Government		
Federal*	**Provincial**	**Municipal**
Parliament Buildings	Provincial Parliament Building	City Hall
House of Commons	Provincial Parliament	City Councillors
Prime Minister	Members of Provincial legislature	Mayor

*students may also write in Members of Parliament (MPs), Opposition or Speaker of the House

Exercise 2
a. Hassan and Ana   b. Yoko and Ana   c. Ana

Challenge
a. Jean Chrétien
b. Roméo Leblanc
c., d., e., f., answers will vary.

Page 115–116 Canadian History Timeline

Exercise 1
a. Vikings reach Canada
b. John Cabot reaches Canada
c. Battle of the Plains of Abraham
d. Confederation is established
e. Red River Rebellion
f. Gold rush in British Columbia
g. Canada gets its own flag
h. Constitution and Charter of Rights signed

Exercise 2
1. Manitoba
2. British Columbia
3. Prince Edward Island
4. Yukon Territory
5. Alberta and Saskatchewan
6. Newfoundland and Labrador
7. Nunavut

Exercise 3
a. 3   b. 1   c. 2   d. 6   e. 5   f. 4

Exercise 4
a. Canada's first prime minister, John A. Macdonald
b. Centennial celebrations at the Parliament buildings
c. Mounties
d. Canadian soldiers in World War I
e. Chinese workers on the Canadian Pacific Railroad
f. the Canadarm

Page 117   Geography

Exercise 1
Land:
rain forest   mountain peak
desert   mountain range
sand dune   hills
peninsula   canyon
island   valley
beach   plains/prairies
forest   meadow
shore

Water:
waterfall   bay
river   lake
ocean   pond

Exercise 2
a. island   f. river
b. mountain peak   g. ocean
c. desert   h. waterfall
d. peninsula
e. lake

Page 118   Mathematics

Exercise 1
a. Operations, trigonometry
b. Shapes, parallel
c. Parts of a circle, angle
d. Types of math, multiplication
e. Solids, square
f. Lines, pyramid
g. Parts of a square, cube
h. Answers (to problems), algebra

Exercise 2
a. circle   d. square   g. triangle
b. cylinder   e. curve   h. pyramid
c. oval   f. cube   i. sphere

Page 119   Science

Exercise 1
a. True   b. False   c. False   d. False

Exercise 2

1.	balances	0
2.	beakers	2
3.	Bunsen burners	1
4.	crucible tongs	2
5.	dissection kits	0
6.	droppers	0
7.	forceps	1
8.	funnels	0
9.	graduated cylinders	0
10.	magnets	0
11.	microscopes	1
12.	Petri dishes	2
13.	slides	3
14.	test tubes	6

Challenge
b. The chemistry teacher is using a Bunsen burner.
c. The physics teacher is writing a formula on the board.
d. A molecule of water has three atoms.

Page 120   Music

Exercise 1
a. violin, cello, bass, guitar, (piano)
b. piano, electric keyboard, accordion, organ

Exercise 2
a. 3   b. 1   c. 6   d. 4   e. 5   f. 2

Page 121 More School Subjects

Exercise 1
a. economics
b. art
c. foreign language
d. computer science
e. business education
f. choir
g. theatre arts
h. Phys. ed./physical education

Exercise 2
Mon.: Phys. ed.
Tues.: English as a second language
Wed.: shop
Thurs.: computer science
Fri.: choir

Pages 122 and 123
North America and Central America

Exercise 1
a. *Possible answers:* New York, Maine, Vermont, Minnesota, North Dakota, Montana, Washington, Idaho, Michigan, Pennsylvania, New Hampshire, Alaska
b. Québec, Ontario, Manitoba, Nunavut
c. Baja California Norte, Sonora, Chihuahua, Coahuila, Tamaulipas
d. Guatemala, El Salvador, Honduras, Nicaragua, Costa Rica, Panama
e. *Possible answers:* Cuba, Jamaica, Haiti and the Dominican Republic/Hispaniola, Puerto Rico, Lesser Antilles

Exercise 2
a. Prince Edward Island
b. Yukon Territory
c. Newfoundland and Labrador
d. Alaska
e. Washington

Exercise 3
a. east
b. west
c. east
d. south
e. north
f. east
g. north
h. northeast
i. southwest

Exercise 4
a. 5,A
b. 6,B
c. 2,C
d. 3,C
e. 1,A
f. 4,B

Pages 124 and 125 The World

Exercise 1
a. Chile
b. Poland
c. Kazakhstan
d. Peru
e. Guatemala
f. Romania
g. Turkey

Exercise 2
1. Pakistan
2. Mexico
3. Italy
4. South Korea
5. Argentina
6. Kenya
7. Iraq
8. Belarus

Exercise 3
a. 5: Moldova, Bulgaria, Ukraine, Serbia, Hungary
b. 3: Brazil, Argentina, Bolivia
c. 6: Libya, Sudan, Central African Republic, Cameroon, Nigeria, Niger
d. 4: Laos, Cambodia, Malaysia, Myanmar
e. 3: United States, Belize, Guatemala

Exercise 4
a. 3   b. 2   c. 4   d. 1

Page 126 Energy and the Environment

Exercise 1
Atoms: nuclear
Air: wind
The Earth: natural gas, geothermal, coal, oil/petroleum
Water: hydroelectric
The Sun: solar

Exercise 2
1. f   2. a   3. e   4. c   5. d   6. b

Exercise 3
a. saving energy
b. saving water
c. recycling
d. saving energy

Page 127 The Universe

Exercise 1
a. False   b. True   c. False   d. True   e. False

Exercise 2
Mercury
Venus
Earth
Mars
Jupiter
Saturn
Uranus
Neptune
Pluto

a. Mercury
b. Pluto
c. Jupiter
d. Saturn
e. Neptune
f. Earth

UNIT 10

Page 128 Trees and Plants

Exercise 1
a. True   b. True   c. False   d. True   e. False
f. True   g. False   h. False   i. True

Exercise 2
1. Sitka spruce
2. oak
3. elm
4. pine
5. palm
6. maple
7. willow
8. dogwood

Page 129 Flowers

Exercise 1
a. pink
b. white and yellow
c. purple
d. red
e. white
f. white
g. yellow
h. pink

Exercise 2
Above the ground: bud, leaf, petal, stem, thorn
Below the ground: bulb, root, seed

Exercise 3
a. 3   b. 2   c. 1   d. 5   e. 4

Pages 130 and 131
Marine Life, Amphibians, and Reptiles

Exercise 1
a. Reptiles, seal
b. Parts of a fish, scallop
c. Amphibians, shark
d. Sea mammals, lizard
e. Sea animals, whale

Exercise 2
a. octopus
b. cod
c. cobra
d. dolphin
e. eel
f. crab
g. seal
h. garter snake

Exercise 3

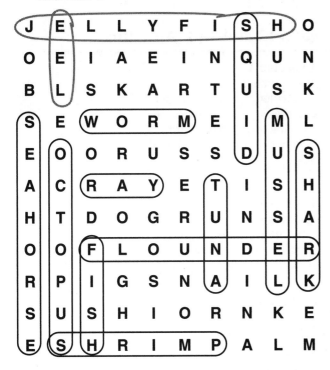

Page 132 Birds, Insects, and Arachnids

Exercise 1
a. robin
b. blue jay
c. eagle
d. owl
e. pigeon
f. hummingbird
g. goose
h. woodpecker
i. duck
j. sparrow

Exercise 2
Items checked:
bee
butterfly
fly
grasshopper
ladybug
spider

Page 133
Domestic Animals and Rodents

Exercise 1
a. squirrel
b. sheep
c. groundhog
d. goat
e. donkey

Exercise 2
Items checked:
goldfish
dog
parakeet
snake
cat
guinea pig
hamster
rabbit
turtle
ferret

Page 134 and 135 Mammals

Exercise 1
a. True   b. False   c. False   d. True   e. True

Exercise 2
a. deer, antlers
b. camel, hump
c. monkey, tail
d. elephant, tusks
e. porcupine, quills
f. lion, paws
g. kangaroo, pouch
h. skunk's, coat

Exercise 3
Items checked:
red wolf
armadillo
panda
gorilla
fox
tiger
zebra
brown bear
camel
grey bat
leopard
elephant
black rhinoceros
kangaroo

UNIT 11

Pages 136 and 137
Jobs and Occupations, A–H

Exercise 1
a. commercial fisher
b. gas station attendant
c. delivery person
d. caregiver/babysitter
e. cook
f. accountant
g. businessman/businesswoman

Exercise 2
a. 4 b. 5 c. 8 d. 1 e. 3 f. 7
g. 6 h. 2

Exercise 3
(Answers may vary slightly.)

Food:
baker
butcher
commercial fisher
cook
homemaker

Clothing:
garment worker

Health:
dental assistant
dentist
doctor
homecare worker

Housing:
architect
bricklayer
carpenter
gardener

Exercise 4
a. cashier
b. cook
c. carpenter
d. dentist, computer programmer
e. auto mechanic
f. firefighter, doctor

Pages 138 and 139
Jobs and Occupations, H–W

Exercise 1
a. False b. ? c. False d. True e. True f. True
g. False h. ? i. False

Exercise 2
a. 5 b. 8 c. 7 d. 3 e. 1 f. 2
g. 4 h. 6

Exercise 3
a. nurse
b. teacher
c. messenger
d. receptionist
e. store owner's
f. telemarketer
g. reporter
h. welder

Exercise 4
a. Ari
b. Chris
c. Mia
d. Luisa
e. Dave
f. Tom

Page 140 Job Skills

Exercise 1
a. Manager, supervise
b. Caregiver, take care of small children, speak English and Spanish
c. Orderly, assist medical patients
d. Assembler, assemble telephone parts
e. Salesperson, sell cars
f. Secretary, work on a computer, type
g. Chef, cook
h. Server, wait on customers

Page 141 Job Search

Exercise 1
Name: <u>Dan King</u>   Job applying for: <u>cashier</u>
1. How did you hear about this job?
   ☑ friends ☑ classifieds ☐ school counsellor
   ☑ job board ☑ help wanted sign
2. Hours:
   ☐ part-time ☑ full-time
3. Have you had any experience? ☑ Yes ☐ No
   If yes, where? <u>a market in China</u>
4. References <u>Sam Parker, Manager, Shopmark</u>
   <u>Supermarket</u>
Interviewed by: <u>Mr Hill</u>
Hired? ☑ Yes ☐ No   Salary: <u>$9 an hour</u>

Exercise 2
a. 3 b. 4 c. 5 d. 2 e. 1

Pages 142 and 143 An Office

Exercise 1
Items circled:
typewriter
calculator
stacking tray
supply cabinet
paper cutter
fax machine
clipboard
paper shredder

Exercise 2
a. 6 b. 1 c. 2 d. 5 e. 4 f. 3

Exercise 3
a. postal scale
b. rotary card file/computer
c. calculator/computer
d. desk calendar/computer/calendar

Exercise 4
1 clipboard
6 bottles of correction fluid
4 bottles of rubber cement
2 bottles of glue
2 boxes of paper clips
3 boxes of push pins
4 rolls of packing tape
5 rolls of clear tape
2 ink pads
4 notepads
3 legal pads
4 typewriter cartridges
2 staplers
3 rubber stamps
1 bag of rubber bands

Page 144 Computers

Exercise 1
Items underlined:
computer   modem
(processor)   keyboard
memory*   mouse
hard (disk) drive software
monitor   printer
CD-ROM (drive)
*in More Vocabulary section of the Dictionary

Exercise 2
a. printer   b. surge protector
c. scanner   d. modem
e. disks/floppies f. laptop
g. cable   h. trackball

Page 145 A Hotel

Exercise 1
a. room service   d. bell captain
b. housekeeper   e. guest
c. valet parking   f. desk clerk

Exercise 2
a. 3   b. 6   c. 5   d. 7   e. 1   f. 2
g. 4

Page 146 A Factory

Exercise 1
a. True b. False c. True d. False e. False

Exercise 2
a. forklift b. time clock c. order picker d. parts

Exercise 3
a. designer   d. shipping clerk
b. line supervisor e. order picker
c. factory worker   f. packer

Challenge
b. The factory owner is in the front office.
d. The line supervisor and shipping clerk have clipboards.
e. There are four boxes on the hand truck.

Page 147 Job Safety

Exercise 1
a. engineer, firefighter   c. machine operator
b. dental assistant, dentist d. movers

Exercise 2
a. warning poison   b. caution explosive
c. danger flammable d. caution corrosive
e. warning flammable f. danger poison

Exercise 3
1. b   2. a   3. c   4. a, d

Exercise 4
a. ears, respirator
b. head, back support
c. eyes, fire extinguisher
d. foot/feet, safety vest

Page 148 Farming and Ranching

Exercise 1
a. orchard   c. field   e. corral
b. barn   d. vineyard f. horse

Exercise 2
a. 3   b. 1   c. 2   d. 4

Page 149 Construction

Exercise 1
Heavy machines:
cherry picker   bulldozer
backhoe   crane

Tools:
jackhammer/ pneumatic drill   shovel
trowel   sledgehammer
pickaxe

Building material:
concrete   insulation   wood/lumber
I-beam/girder stucco   drywall
bricks   plywood   shingles

Exercise 2
a. 5   b. 4   c. 2   d. 3   e. 1

Challenge

Possible answers:

One construction worker is using a jackhammer/pneumatic drill.

Two construction workers are pushing/holding an I beam/girder.

One is measuring something.

One is in a cherry picker/drilling something.

One is driving a backhoe.

One is driving a bulldozer.

One is operating a crane.

One is carrying a tool box.

Two are putting up scaffolding.

Two are supervising/planning.

Pages 150 and 151
Tools and Building Supplies

Exercise 1
a. outlet   c. hammer   e. drill bit
b. axe   d. chisel   f. flashlight

Exercise 2
a. electrical tape   e. drill bit
b. Phillips screwdriver   f. scraper
c. screwdriver   g. sandpaper
d. level   h. battery

Exercise 3
a. 6   b. 4   c. 2   d. 5   e. 3   f. 1

Exercise 4
a. True   b. False   c. False   d. True   e. False
f. False   g. True

UNIT 12

Page 152 Place to Go

Exercise 1
a. gardener   b. announcer   c. zookeeper

Exercise 2
Words circled:

art gallery   Flea Market
paintings   County Fair
puppet show   exhibitions
Amusement Park   prizes
Carnival   Zoo
baseball game   Botanical Gardens
seats   the Movies

Exercise 3
a. zoo   e. flea market
b. movies   f. carnival
c. art gallery   g. botanical gardens
d. baseball game   h. amusement park

Page 153 The Park and Playground

Exercise 1
a. picnic table   c. bike path
b. ball field   d. water fountain/picnic table

Exercise 2

Legend:
tennis court
playground
ball field
duck pond
bike path
picnic table
water fountain

Exercise 3
a. True   b. False   c. False   d. True   e. False

Page 154 Outdoor Recreation

Exercise 1
a. 2   b. 1   c. 2   d. 4*   e. 2   f. 1
g. 3   h. 3**   i. 1
*or 5, including the boy fishing
**or 5, including the hikers

Exercise 2
a. lantern   f. life vest
b. matches   g. camping stove
c. canteen   h. sleeping bag
d. multi-use knife   i. foam pad
e. insect repellent   j. fishing rod

Page 155 The Beach

Exercise 1
a. sand
b. beach towel, beach chair
c. cooler
d. sunscreen/sunblock, beach umbrella
e. wet suit
f. scuba tank

Exercise 2
a. True   b. True   c. False   d. True   e. False   f. False

Pages 156 and 157 Sports Verbs

Exercise 1
a. 5   b. 1   c. 3   d. 2   e. 4

Exercise 2
a. jog   d. swim   g. ski
b. ride a bike   e. run
c. walk   f. skate

Exercise 3
a. Two women are running in the park. False
b. A man is dribbling the ball. False
c. A woman is stretching. True
d. A girl is diving into the ocean. False
e. A man is tackling two men. False
f. Three men are racing. True
g. A man is pitching a ball. True

Exercise 4
a. swim	c. kick	e. bend
b. finish	d. pitch	f. serve

Challenge
a. One woman is running in the park./ Two women are walking in the park.
b. A woman/girl is dribbling the ball.
d. A girl is diving into a swimming pool.
e. A man is tackling another/one man.

Page 158 Team Sports

Exercise 1
a. 2   b. 12   c. 2   d. 2   e. 1   f. 0 to 0

Exercise 2
a. football	b. volleyball	c. soccer
d. baseball	e. basketball	

Challenge
basketball: 5	baseball: 9	football: 11
soccer: 11	ice hockey: 6	volleyball: 6*

*in some forms of the game, 4 or 2

Page 159 Individual Sports

Exercise 1
Hit a ball: billiards/pool, table tennis/Ping-Pong™, golf, tennis, racquetball
Ride: cycling/biking, horse racing
Throw something: track and field, flying disc
Lift something: weightlifting
Use a target: archery
Stand on wheels: inline skating, skateboarding
Wear a mask: fencing
Wear a leotard: gymnastics

Exercise 2
1. bowling	4. tennis
2. cycling/biking	5. racquetball
3. golf	6. table tennis/Ping-Pong™

Page 160
Winter Sports and Water Sports

Exercise 1
a. cross-country skiing	c. windsurfing
b. sledding	d. scuba diving

Exercise 2
a. Caribe Plaza or Mirror Lake Inn	e. Wicker Inn
b. Hillside Lodge or Wicker Inn	f. Mirror Lake Inn
c. Hillside Lodge	g. Caribe Plaza
d. Caribe Plaza	h. Mirror Lake Inn

Page 161 Sports Equipment

Exercise 1
Baseball:	Football:	Skiing:	Archery:
bat	helmet	boots	bow
catcher's mask	shoulder pads	poles	arrow
glove			target
uniform			

Golf:	Tennis:	Skating:	Soccer:
club	racquet	inline skates	shin guards

Exercise 2
a. basketballs	d. tennis racquets
b. hockey sticks	e. golf clubs
c. soccer balls	

Challenge
Possible answers:
basketball	baseball bat	hockey stick
uniforms	football helmet	shin guards
catcher's mask	football	volleyball
glove	shoulder pads	
baseball	soccer ball	

Pages 162 and 163
Hobbies and Games

Exercise 1
a. clay	c. figurines	e. dice
b. clubs	d. crochet	f. glue

Exercise 4
a. board game	e. paper doll
b. video game	f. clay
c. yarn	g. cartridge
d. figurine	

Letters in circles: BEDMRIROYE
Unscrambled word: embroidery

Exercise 5
a. paper doll	b. clay
c. board game	d. yarn

Pages 164 and 165
Electronics and Photography

Exercise 1
a. microphone
b. right
c. below
d. above
e. on
f. headphones
g. left
h. on
i. video camera

Exercise 2
a. $27
b. $10
c. $31
d. $150
e. $11
f. $18
g. $13
h. $21

Exercise 3
a. rewind
b. fast forward
c. stop
d. pause
e. record
f. play

Exercise 4
a. 1 b. 3 c. 4 d. 5 e. 2

Pages 166 and 167 Entertainment

Exercise 1
Items circled:

stand-up comedy
talk show
soap opera
movie
comedy
news
movie
action-adventure
television program
opera
nature program
mystery
news
movie
romance
play
ballet
game show
cartoon
movie
horror

Exercise 2
a. 8:00, Channel 2
b. 10:00, Channel 6
c. 8:00, Channel 5
d. 9:00, Channel 2
e. 10:00, Channel 4
f. 10:00, Channel 5
g. 8:00, Channel 6
h. 11:00, Channel 2; 11:00, Channel 5
i. 8:30, Channel 5; 9:00, Channel 7

Exercise 4
a. quiz show
b. shopping program
c. western
d. children's program
e. science fiction story
f. soap opera
g. tragedy
h. concert

Page 168 Holidays

Exercise 1
a. Canada Day
b. Valentine's Day
c. Halloween
d. New Year's Day
e. Christmas
f. Thanksgiving

Exercise 2
a. New Year, New Year's Day
b. Halloween, jack-o'-lantern
c. Thanksgiving, turkey, feast
d. Valentine's Day, heart
e. Christmas, tree, ornaments

Page 169 A Party

Exercise 1
a. Tom
b. The guests
c. Sue
d. Tom
e. Tom
f. The guests (and Tom)
g. Tom
h. The guests (and Tom)
i. Sue
j. Sue

Exercise 2
Items crossed out:
invite guests
buy candles
buy gift
buy card

Page 170 Another Look (Unit 1)

Possible circled items:

coins
classroom
chalkboard
chalk
circle
conversation
clock
colours
cardinal numbers
calendar
cloudy
cold
computer
chair
cassette player
cellular phone
Celsius

Page 171 Another Look (Unit 2)

Page 172 Another Look (Unit 3)

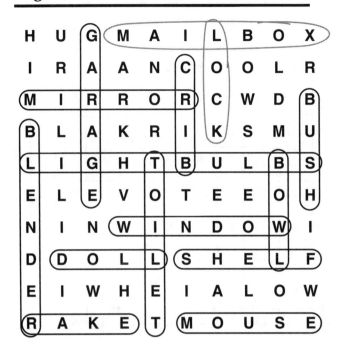

Page 173 Another Look (Unit 4)

Possible circled items:

coconut	coleslaw
cantaloupe	can
cherries	colander
container	can opener
carrots	chili pepper
chicken	corn
cutting board	catfish
chef	cookies
carving knife	(chocolate) cake
corned beef	coffee pot
cheese	(coffee) cups
casserole	celery
cucumbers	crab
cauliflower	cheeseburger
cabbage	

Page 174 Another Look (Unit 5)

Page 175 Another Look (Unit 6)

Page 176 Another Look (Unit 7)

Possible circled items:

coffee shop	church
(coffee) cup	court(room)
candy store	car
cart	car accident
card store	crosswalk
CDs	convenience store
curb	copy centre
corner	

Page 177 Another Look (Unit 8)

(Answers may vary slightly.)
on the bus
in the passenger's hand
on the luggage carrier/ cart
near the train track
on the bridge
in the convertible/car
on the licence plate
under the car
on the airplane
at/by the street vendor
on the stop sign
in the pickup truck

Page 178 Another Look (Unit 9)

English Composition:
paragraph, sentence, colon, edit

Math: square, cube, diameter, algebra

Music: flute, piano, trumpet, accordion

Geography: island, ocean, river, plains

Science: slide, atom, prism, chemistry

The Universe: telescope, Mercury, galaxy, constellation

Page 179 Another Look [Unit 10]

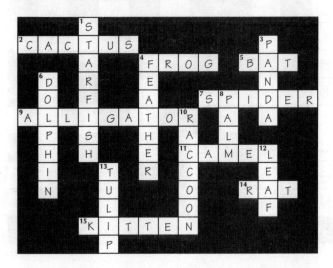

Page 180 Another Look [Unit 11]

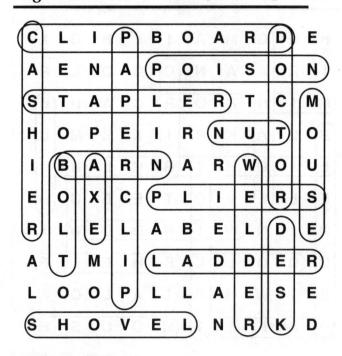

Page 181 Another Look (Unit 12)

Possible circled items:

camping	cards
campfire	concert
camping stove	camcorder
cooler	cycling
canoe	castle
canteen	collect/collecting
camera	canvas
camera case	catcher's mask
climbing	catch/catching
(clown) costume	clubs
cartoon	coach
clock radio	chess